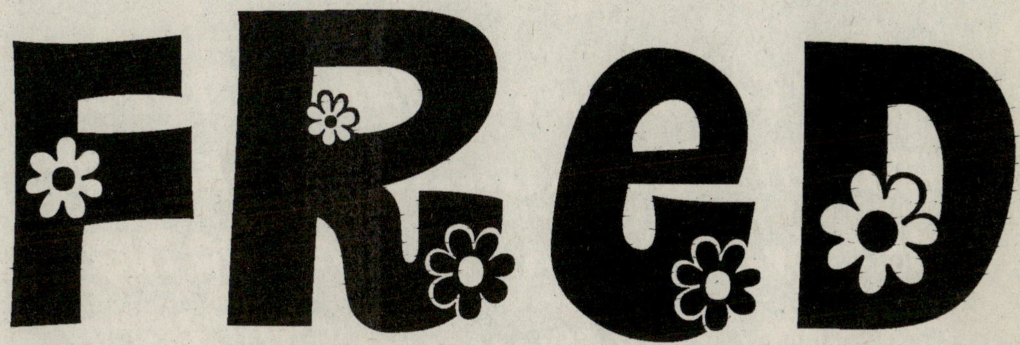

The POSSeSSeD FLOWeR

"TO HELL IN A FLOWER BASKET!!!"

✿ ✿ ✿ ✿ ✿ ✿

HAPPY PREDATOR PUBLICATIONS

Creator-Writer-Illustrator
HAPPY NICK HARDCASTLE

Editor .... STEVAN CVJETKOVICH

HPP Logo Painted by........... J.R. NEWTON

Photos by................. SANDRO TUCCI

Computer Design by.......... SWAC MEDIA

Business Co-ordinator........EDGAR FRONT

Submissions Editor........HEATHER HARRIS

Visit us online at http://
www. happypredator.com

 HAPPY PREDATOR PUBLICATIONS 52 Carrier Drive, Unit 12, Etobicoke, Ontario, Canada M9W 5S5. For information on: advertising, promotions and licensing call (416) 753-8252 or fax (416) 798-2086. For new project updates or back orders visit us online at www.happypredator.com

ISBN 0-9685626-0-4

Printed in Canada

In memory of BIG KITTY

"HAPPY AND FRED HAVE CORNERED THE MARKET ON ANGER AND AS EVERYONE SHOULD KNOW, I FEEL ANGER IS A GIFT, SO WHY NOT USE IT? THANK YOU HAPPY FOR YOUR DEMENTED AND TORTURED RAMBLINGS."

... EDGE

"HAPPY AND FRED CAN RUN WITH US ANYTIME 'CAUSE JUST LIKE THE BROOD, THEY'RE NOT EXACTLY THE FAMILY NEXT DOOR."

... CHRISTIAN

"THE BROOD FINALLY HAVE COMPANY ON THE DARK AND DESOLATE PLAINS OF HELL. HAPPY AND FRED CAN DRINK FROM OUR CUP ANY TIME."

... GANGREL

THE BROOD, WWF

FRED THE POSSESSED FLOWER in...
"TO HELL IN A FLOWER BASKET"

THE PREMISE...

WHEN PEOPLE HEAR FAIRY TALES, TYPICAL CANDY COATED IMAGES COME TO MIND. HOW IN FACT DOES A JOLLY, FAT MAN KNOW IF WE HAVE BEEN NAUGHTY OR NICE? WHY ARE TRIPPY, CHOCOLATE EGG LAYING RABBITS SO SOCIALLY ACCEPTABLE? WOULD YOU BE TOTALLY AT EASE KNOWING THAT SOMEONE HAS BROKEN INTO YOUR HOUSE AND HAS REPLACED YOUR CHILD'S TOOTH WITH SOME POCKET CHANGE? DO YOU REALLY WANT TO KNOW WHAT MYSTERIOUS SOUL WRITES THESE TALES?

PICTURE, IF YOU WILL, TWO RIVAL COMPANIES *(HEAVEN AND HELL)*, NOT GOOD AND NOT EVIL BUT RATHER BRAND "Y" AND BRAND "X", EACH COMPETING FOR SPIRITUAL MARKET SHARE. JUST IMAGINE THE ADVERTISING CAMPAIGNS AND MARKETING STRATEGIES INVOLVED IN RUNNING THESE CELESTIAL CONGLOMORATES!

WHO IS FRED THE POSSESSED FLOWER?!

IF HELL WAS WKRP AND THE DEVIL WAS ARTHUR CARLSON... THEN FRED WOULD DEFINETLY BE ANDY TRAVIS. FRED HANDLES ALL OF THE SINFUL PROMOTIONS FOREVER INCREASING THE UNDERWORLDS CUSTOMER BASE; HE NEGOCIATES DEALS FOR THE DEVIL AND BASICALLY IS IN CHARGE OF CORPORATE HELL. IN SHORT, FRED IS THE COAT HANGER OF EVIL, HOLDING THE MUFFLER OF DEBAUCHARY FIRMLY IN PLACE... THE DEVIL IS JUST THE SPOKESPERSON, FRED IS *DEE-MON!!!*

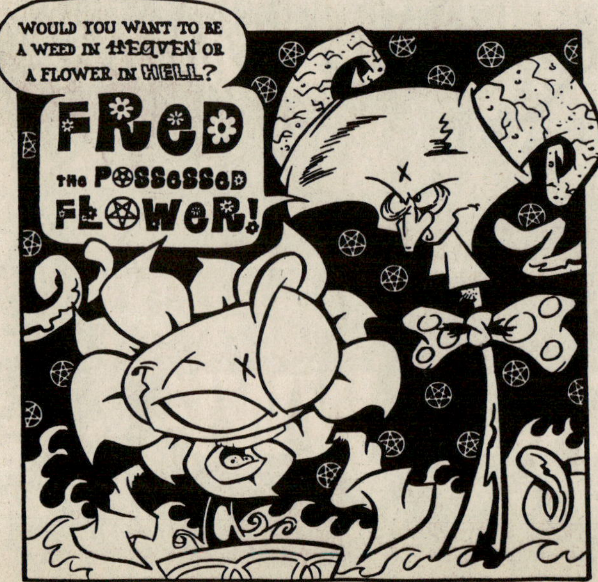

HELL'S FLUNKIES...

NEW CHARACTERS! I DON'T THINK SO... EVERY SUPPORTING CAST MEMBER IS A RELIGIOUS OR FOLK ICON, 666 TIMES MORE FAMOUS THEN ANY PIDDLY, LITTLE CARTOON CHARACTERS SUCH AS MICKEY OR THE MAN OF STEEL!

LUCIFER The X-Angel (LOUIE): WHAT A SATANIC SIMPLETON!!! JUST BECAUSE YOU ARE THE OWNER OF HELL AND JUST BECAUSE YOU MAKE A GREAT SPOKESPERSON... DOESN'T MEAN THAT YOU KNOW HOW TO RUN A DAMNED COMPANY. NO PUN INTENDED.

CUPID: THIS SHIFTY, COSMIC FREELANCER SPECIALIZES IN PROMISCUITY, MIND GAMES AND IS AN ALL AROUND SUPERFREAK. BUT HEY, WHAT'S LOVE GOTTA DO WITH IT?!

BOOGIEMAN: DEMONIC, EBONIC, SARDONIC, MORONIC AND WITH ONE HARSH SCARE YOU MIGHT NEED A COLONIC!

TOOTHFAIRY: THIS TEMPERMENTAL TINKERBELL CONTRADICTS EVERY UHHH... CONTRADICTION IN THE BOOK! JUST PICTURE A FAT GUY IN DRAG, WITH WINGS?

A HELL OF A LOT MORE...

FILLING IN ALL THE CELESTIAL POTHOLES ARE GUEST CHARACTERS SUCH AS THE BIG GUY (GOD), AND HIS SIDEKICK - THE BURNING HEDGE, THE EASTER BUNNY, THE FOUR HORSEMEN, THE ANGEL MICHEAL, GRETCHEN (HELL'S SEXY SECRETARY) AND FATE'S CELESTIAL BUSINESS CONTROL BOARD BASED IN PURGATORY!

SEE THE BIG GUY AND LUCIFER PLAY GOLF TOGETHER, HELL'S WORKERS UNION GOES ON STRIKE, THE UNHOLY FLOWER FALLS IN LOVE, HELL'S INTERNAL FINANCIAL AUDIT, DISCOVER THAT GOD IS A CHICK, JESUS WAS BLACK AND MANY OTHER TWISTED TALES OF UNCOMFORTABLY ACCURATE SOCIAL PARODY!!!

FRED THE POSSESD FLOWER IS FAST PACED AND REVEALS MANY TRUTHS ABOUT THE CORPORATE WORLD WE LIVE IN. THE THIRTEEN UNLUCKY TALES THAT YOU ARE ABOUT TO READ MOCKS LIFE AND THE WEB WE WEAVE.

IT WOULD BE A SIN NOT TO ENJOY THIS BOOK!!!

SEE YOU IN HELL,
HAPPY NICK HARDCASTLE

HAPPY PREDATOR PUBLICATIONS

HAPPY NICK'S

FRED the POSSESSED FLOWER

1

"THE PLANT BEHIND THE SCENES"

GUEST STARRING: GOD & SATAN

THE PLANT BEHIND THE SCENES

WHEN PEOPLE HEAR FAIRY TALES, TYPICAL, CANDY COATED IMAGES COME TO MIND. HOW IN FACT, DOES A JOLLY, FAT, MAN KNOW IF WE HAVE BEEN NAUGHTY OR NICE? WHY ARE TRIPPY, CHOCOLATE EGG LAYING RABBITS SO SOCIALLY ACCEPTABLE? WOULD YOU BE TOTALLY AT EASE KNOWING THAT SOMEONE HAS BROKEN INTO YOUR HOUSE AND HAD REPLACED YOUR CHILD'S TOOTH WITH SOME POCKET CHANGE? DO YOU REALLY WANT TO KNOW WHAT MYSTERIOUS SOUL WRITES THESE ANONYMOUS TALES?

HELL'S MOUNT RUSHMOORE...

HITLER
NIXON
SADAM
YOKO

WELCOME TO
HELL
POPULATION
666 ZILLION

CREATED,
WRITTEN
and
ILLUSTRATED
by:
HAPPY

HELL'S BREAK ROOM...
HEY CUPID, MY MAN, HOW WAS YOUR DAY?
FREAKIN' LONG, MY WINGS ARE READY TO FALL OFF. WHAT ABOUT YOU, BOOGIEMAN?
SAME JIVE, DIFFERENT DAY. WHAT ABOUT YOU, TOOTH FAIRY?

MY BACK IS SOAR AS HELL FROM LUGGING AROUND SACKS OF TEETH AND POCKET CHANGE ALL DAY.
I DON'T KNOW ABOUT YOU GUYS, BUT I THINK THAT IT'S ABOUT TIME THAT OUR WAGES AND BENEFITS WERE INCREASED!

AMEN!!!

THIS IS CRAZY, WE HAVE GOTTA TALK TO FRED.

I SAY THAT WE GO STRAIGHT TO THE TOP AND TALK TO LOUIE, IN PERSON.
TOOTH FAIRY, ARE YOU NUTS? FRED MANAGES EVERYTHING DOWN HERE. IF WE GO OVER HIS HEAD HE WILL INCINERATE US!

OUTSIDE FRED'S OFFICE...
IN RECEPTION...
EXCUSE ME, FRED... THE TOOTH FAIRY, THE BOOGIEMAN AND CUPID ARE HERE TO SEE YOU.
THANK YOU, GRETCHEN. SEND THEM IN.

FRED'S OFFICE...
WHAT CAN I DO FOR YOU BOYS?
WE WOULD AHH...
LIKE A LITTLE MORE AHH...
AHH... PAY.

SERIOUSLY?... WELL GUYS I'M SORRY, BUT THE COMPANY CAN'T AFFORD IT RIGHT NOW.

IN THAT CASE WE WOULD LIKE TO SPEAK WITH THE OWNER.

LOUIE IS UNAVAILABLE. AND IF YOU DON'T LIKE YOUR SITUATION WHY DON'T YOU GO WORK FOR THE BIG GUY? YOU KNOW?... **LEAD YOURSELF OUT OF TEMPTATION AND DELIVER YOURSELVES FROM EVIL.**

WE USED TO WORK FOR HIM BUT HE WAS REALLY CHEAP. ALL THAT WE GOT PAID WAS OUR OWN SELF-FULFILLMENT. WHO CAN LIVE ON THAT?

YA, THAT IS WHY WE STARTED FREELANCING FOR LOUIE IN THE FIRST PLACE. BUT NOW THAT WE ARE UNION, WE WILL STRIKE IF WE DON'T GET WHAT WE WANT.

I DON'T KNOW HOW SANTA AND THE EASTER BUNNY STILL DO IT, ESPECIALLY WITH ALL OF THEIR OVERHEAD COSTS.

HELL'S SPA...
LOOK LOUIE, WE CAN'T AFFORD TO PAY OUR EMPLOYEES MORE, EVER SINCE PURGATORY STARTED OFFERING LOWER HOLY REDEMPTION RATES ON HEAVENLY ADMITTANCE.
THE BIG GUY IS USING A LOST LEADER TO PUT ME OUT OF BUSINESS?
EXACTLY! ONCE YOU ARE OUT OF THE PICTURE THE BIG GUY CAN MAKE UP HIS MINOR LOSSES AND OVER FILL HIS QUOTA DUE TO HIS NEWLY ACQUIRED MONOPOLY.
WHILE WE ARE TEMPORARILY WITHOUT STAFF I WILL NEED YOU TO DO MORE FIELD WORK AND TO SPEND LESS TIME IN THE OFFICE.
YOU WANT ME TO GO PUBLIC? BUT I AM A BEHIND THE SCENES GUY. I RUN EVERYTHING FROM AN EXECUTIVE, INTERNAL LEVEL. BESIDES, I HATE PEOPLE. THAT IS WHY I WORK FOR YOU.
THOSE ARE THE EXACT REASONS I NEED YOU TO BE MY NEW FIELD AGENT.

IF I WERE TO FILL IN, I WOULD BE A SCAB.
WHY CAN'T I HEAD UP THE SEARCH FOR REPLACEMENT WORKERS AND JUST TEACH SOME SEMINARS, OR SOMETHING?
THERE IS NO TIME. YOU KNOW ALL OF THE INS AND OUTS OF ALL THE DIFFERENT FIELD AGENTS JOBS. THIS IS ONLY A TEMPORARY ASSIGNMENT. THE BIG GUY CAN'T KEEP UP THESE LOW RATE DEALS FOR LONG. WE JUST HAVE TO SURVIVE LONG ENOUGH FOR HIM TO EXHAUST HIS LOST LEADER PROMOTION.
YOU ARE THE SMARTEST RIGHT HAND MAN THAT I HAVE EVER HAD. YOU ARE HELL'S MANAGER, I AM JUST THE OWNER.
I AM ACCUSTOMED TO A CERTAIN LIFESTYLE. I'M TOO WEAK TO LOSE EVERYTHING! I CAN'T START FROM SCRATCH ALL OVER AGAIN!
PLEASE! PLEASE! PLEASE!
OK, OK... JUST CUT THAT OUT. I CAN'T STAND TO SEE A GROWN DEVIL CRY.
SOMEWHERE OVER SOCIETY...
WHOOSH!

POP!

Hi!

OK, LET'S SEE WHAT'S FIRST ON THE AGENDA. ASSIGNMENT NUMBER ONE, FOR CUPID... MAKE A COUPLE OF STRANGERS FALL IN LOVE BLA, BLA, BLA TIME, ADDRESS ETC. PIECE OF CAKE.

THERE IS THE LUCKY COUPLE NOW...
WAIT A SECOND...
THERE IS A MISTAKE; THE STRANGERS SHOULD BE WALKING ON THE SAME SIDE OF THE STREET SO THAT THEY CAN BUMP INTO EACH OTHER...
THOSE IDIOTS IN THE FATE DEPT!

I HAD BETTER PUT THIS THING TO THE MAXIMUM SETTING JUST TO BE SAFE.
HATE...
TOLERATE...
LIKE...
LOVE...
SUPER FREAK SEX SLAVE!!!
ZOOM!!!
ZING!
ZING!
ZING!

WHAAA?!
SUGAR LUMPS!!!
POOKIE PIE!!!
HONEY WOOKUMS!!!
I'M COMING
LAMB CHOP!!!

BAM!!!

CUP CAKE?...

I LOVE THOSE GUYS
IN THE FATE DEPT.
WHAT A SENSE OF HUMOR...
WELL, THIS ISN'T AS BAD AS
I THOUGHT IT WOULD BE.

NEXT ON THE AGENDA...
SUBURBIA...
ALL RIGHT, THIS IS THE PLACE. I JUST HAVE TO REPLACE ONE STUPID, LITTLE TOOTH WITH SOME CHANGE AND THAT WILL TAKE CARE OF MY DUTIES AS THE TOOTH FAIRY FOR THIS EVENING.
?
HOW THE HELL AM I GOING TO GET UP TO THAT DAMN KID'S WINDOW?
POLEVAULT!

BOING!
!!
I'M FREEZING.

DAMN!

RAIN...
WHY THAT LITTLE @▯$%&°

NOW I'VE GOT TO FIND ANOTH...
!
SQUAWK!
STUPID BIRD!
SQUAWK!
SQUAWK!
THUD
POP!
HOLY SHEEP!!!

INSIDE THE McPHERSON HOUSEHOLD..
I HOPE THAT LOUIE APPRECIATES WHAT I'M DOING.
GRRRRRRRR!!
HISSSSSSSS!
HEH, HEH.

INSIDE BILLY'S ROOM...
CREEEEEEEK
HORNY THE FISH!
I WISH THAT I HAD TOYS LIKE THIS WHEN I WAS A KID.

SHEESH KABOB
I HOPE THAT THIS TEDDY BEAR CAN HOLD MY WEIGHT.
SNAP!
I'M YOUR FRIEND!
WHAT THE HELL WAS THAT?!
WHO ARE YOU?
DON'T WORRY ABOUT IT KID, YOU'RE DREAMING, JUST GO BACK TO SLEEP.
THERE'S A TALKING FLOWER ON MY BED AND YOU EXPECT ME TO JUST GO BACK TO SLEEP, WHAT ARE YOU, SOME KIND OF A MORON?
H

FINE, IF YOU MUST KNOW, I'M THE TOOTH FAIRY.
NO YOU'RE NOT...
YES I AM.
NO YOU'RE NOT.
YOU'RE A FLOWER.
THE TOOTH FAIRY IS SUPPOSED TO BE NICE. YOU'RE MEAN.
YEA, SO, THAT'S BESIDES THE POINT. I WANT YOUR DAMN TOOTH AND I'M WILLING TO PAY FOR IT... DOESN'T THAT QUALIFY ME TO BE THE FREAKIN' TOOTH FAIRY?
ALRIGHT!!! HAVE IT YOUR WAY. I'M JUST A TEMP, OK...THE REAL TOOTH FAIRY IS IN RE-HAB... HAPPY?
WHATEVER, BUT SINCE YOU'RE NOT THE REAL TOOTH FAIRY, IT'S GONNA COST YOU TRIPLE.
WHY YOU LITTLE **@@/@!!! DID I FORGET TO MENTION THAT I AM ALSO FILLING IN FOR THE BOOGIEMAN!

THAT LITTLE KID IS A TYRANT.
BETTER MAKE A NOTE...
...HE MIGHT JUST HAVE
TO COME WORK FOR ME
ONE OF THESE DAYS.
HA HA HA HA HA HA HA
BUT ANYWAYS...
HEAVEN
IN HEAVEN...

ON THE HOLY BACK NINE
IT LOOKS TO ME LIKE YOUR ASSISTANT IS HAVING A ROUGH TIME ADAPTING TO HIS NEW JOB. BURNING HEDGE, DON'T YOU AGREE?
WHAT EVER YOU SAY, BIG GUY.
DON'T WORRY BIG GUY, HE'S JUST GETTING WARMED UP.

MEANWHILE...
CLICK!
I WONDER HOW FRED IS DOING?

SOMEWHERE IN THE CITY...
I HOPE THAT I AM NOT LATE FOR MY NEXT APPOINTMENT. I HAVE TO SAVE SOME LADY AND SCARE THE CRAP OUT OF TWO SCUMBAGS... THIS LOOKS LIKE A JOB FOR THE
BOOGIEMAN!
HELP!!!...
PERFECT TIMING.
HAND OVER THE PURSE IF YOU KNOW WHAT'S GOOD FOR YOU.
MUAHAHAHAHA!
BACK OFF, LOSERS.

HA HA HA HA HA HA
WHAT THE HELL ARE YOU SUPPOSED TO BE? HA HA.
THE BOOGIE MAN!
OOOOHHHA DON'T SCARE US LIKE THAT MR. ALL-POWERFUL,BOOGIE MAN.
I THOUGHT THAT THE BOOGIE MAN ONLY BUGGED KIDS.
NO, I BUG EVERYONE. I JUST LET THE CHILDREN LIVE TO TELL ABOUT IT.
GO AHEAD & GIVE ME YOUR BEST SHOT.

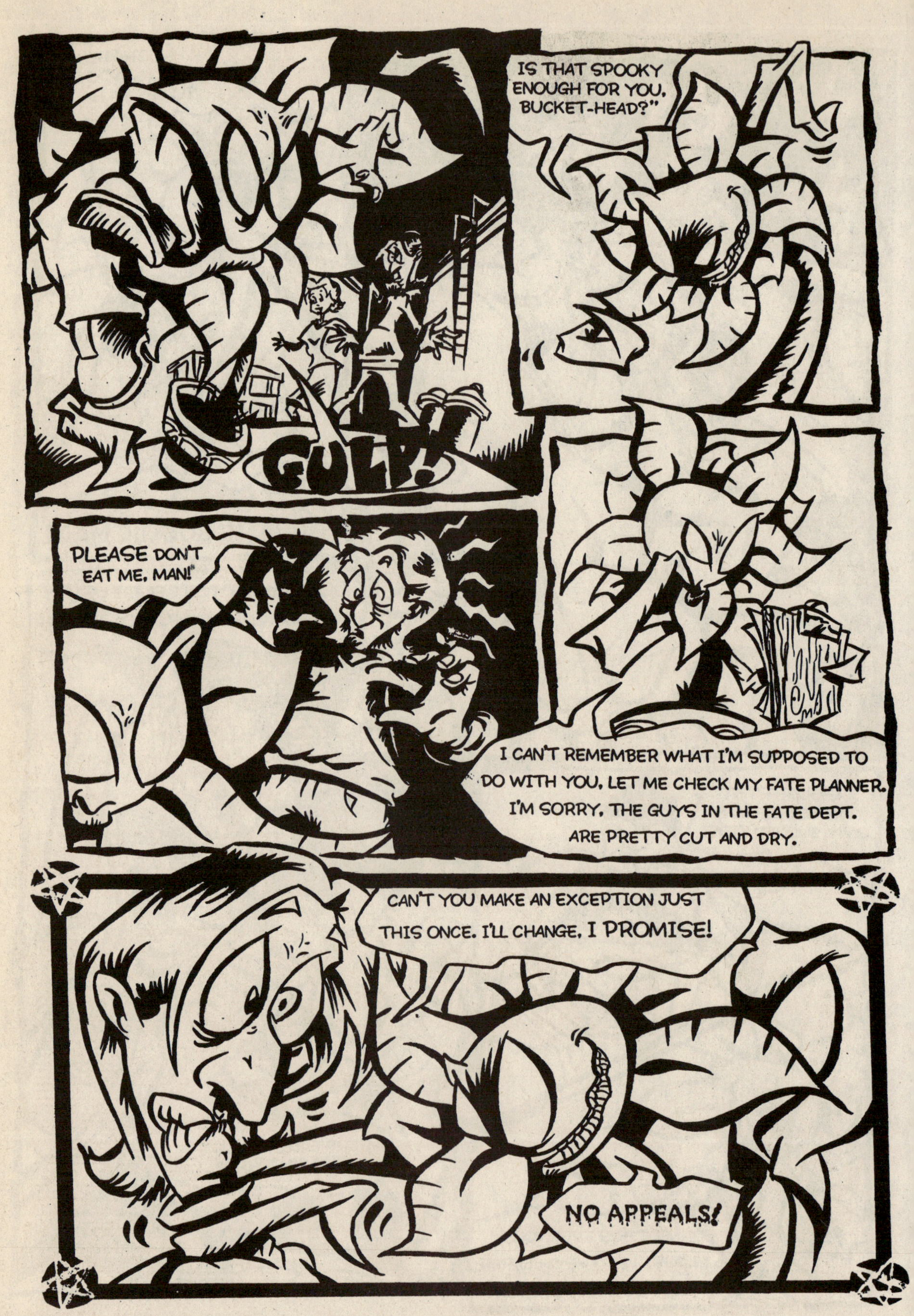
GULP!
IS THAT SPOOKY ENOUGH FOR YOU, BUCKET-HEAD?"
PLEASE DON'T EAT ME, MAN!"
I CAN'T REMEMBER WHAT I'M SUPPOSED TO DO WITH YOU, LET ME CHECK MY FATE PLANNER. I'M SORRY, THE GUYS IN THE FATE DEPT. ARE PRETTY CUT AND DRY.
CAN'T YOU MAKE AN EXCEPTION JUST THIS ONCE. I'LL CHANGE, I PROMISE!
NO APPEALS!

GULP!
YUMMY!
THANK YOU SO MU...
YOU POLLUTE THE ENVIRONMENT WITH YOUR CARS AND CIGARETTES AND SO FORTH. YOU EVEN WEAR REAL FUR COATS, YOU'RE JUST AS HUMAN AS THOSE THUGS. THE ONLY REASON I DON'T SNACK ON YOU TOO IS ONLY BECAUSE YOU'RE NOT ON MY AGENDA...TODAY. NOW BEAT IT.
SHUT UP DUMMY!
OH MY GOD!
OH YOUR GOD, INDEED.

1 (800) 666- HELL
HEY LOUIE, JUST CALLING TO LET YOU KNOW THAT I'VE SENT YOU A COUPLE OF CUSTOMERS.... JUST TRYIN' TO INCREASE SALES.
YOU KNOW. I THINK I COULD GET USED TO THIS NEW JOB. I AM CONFIDENT THAT WE WILL HAVE THIS SITUATION WRAPPED UP IN NO TIME. SEE YOU BACK AT THE OFFICE.
THE END!

HAPPY PREDATOR PUBLICATIONS
HAPPY NICK'S
FRED
2
the POSSESSED FLOWER
"FASTFOOD FOR THE SOUL"
GUEST STARRING: GOD & SATAN

FAST FOOD FOR THE SOUL
THE FORCES OF GOOD AND EVIL ARE TWO RIVAL BUSINESSES CONSTANTLY IN COMPETITION ON A CAPITALISTIC PLAYING FIELD. THIS IS THE TALE OF TWO DIFFERENT BRANDS OF THE SAME PRODUCT CONSTANTLY IMPLEMENTING THE PROMOTIONS OF FATE. WITNESS THE ON GOING BATTLE FOR MARKET SHARE, UTILIZING THE SOULS OF HUMANITY AS CURRENCY, GREEDY JERKS.
FOR PREZ
1992... WASHINGTON...
FREAK The POSSESSED FLOWER
CREATED, WRITTEN and ILLUSTRATED by: HAPPY

1950... HELL'S BOARDROOM...

GOOD AFTERNOON, LOUIE. ESTEEMED MEMBERS OF THE BOARD OF DEMONS.

FAST FOOD WOULD BE A GLOBALLY MARKETED PRODUCT, CATERING TO THE GLUTTONY OF ALL DEMOGRAPHIC AND PSYCHO GRAPHIC GROUPS.
FAST FOOD WILL BE AN APPEALING MEAL WITH MINIMAL NUTRITION CONTENT.
THE OBJECTIVES OF FAST FOOD WILL BE TO INCREASE FAT AND CHOLESTEROL AMONG PEOPLE SO THAT ATTRITION WILL OCCUR PREMATURELY.
THIS WILL ENSURE OUR GOAL OF GENERATING MORE IN STORE TRAFFIC FOR PURGATORY, IN TURN GENERATING MORE CUSTOMERS FOR HELL.

I HAVE PLANNED SEVERAL PRODUCT DEVELOPMENT STRATEGIES TO KEEP FAST FOOD POPULAR FOR THE LONG TERM.
ENVIRONMENTALLY FRIENDLY SUBSTITUTES FOR NON-BIODEGRADABLE, STYROFOAM PACKAGING, EXTRA VALUE ENTREE'S, TWO FOR ONE DEAL, PROMOTIONAL TOYS AND CAMERAS IN THE KITCHENS SO THAT EMPLOYEES CAN'T DO STRANGE THINGS TO THE DEEP FRYER GREASE.
IN CLOSING...
... AN ASSORTMENT OF VARIOUS CANDY COATED, MASCOT TOTING FAST FOOD CHAINS WILL BRING SEVERE WAIT GAIN AND GRIM CHAOS TO CONSUMERS EVERYWHERE!

RENEGADE
BURRITOS

RUN FROM THE BOARDER!
99¢ TACO KID

WING KING

TRY MY NEW JUMBO BUCKET!

GREASSY SPOONS R-US
FAST FOOD FOR THE SOUL...
EAT ME IN ST. LOUIS
DOUBLE CHINS TAKE-OUT
SC SUPER CHEESE PIZZA
ROCK CUISINE FRENCH FRIES
HELL'S KITCHEN

HEAVEN'S HEALTH SPA:..
1980...
THAT'S THE SPOT.
DRINKS ANYONE?
LOUIE, I HAVE BEEN OBSERVING THE PROGRESS OF YOUR FAST FOOD PROMOTION.
SO WHAT DO YOU THINK?

VERY INVENTIVE,
YET RATHER ANNOYING.
SMASH!
YA! IT'S VERY INVENTIVE, BUT RATHER ANNOYING. YOU TELL HIM, BIG GUY.
BURNING HEDGE, THAT'S ENOUGH.
QUITE FRANKLY, I WANT YOU TO RECALL THE FAST FOOD PROMOTION.
BIG GUY, YOU'RE ASKING A LOT. CAN I GET BACK TO YOU?

LOUIE'S BACKYARD...
WE CAN'T LET THE BIG GUY PULL OUR FAST FOOD PROMOTION. IT'S ONE OF OUR BIGGEST MONEYMAKERS.
I JUST DON'T KNOW WHAT COULD HAPPEN IF THE BIG GUY TAKES THINGS INTO HIS OWN HANDS.
WITH THIS MUCH REVENUE AT STAKE, I SAY WE TAKE THAT CHANCE.
OK, FINE. BUT BRAKE IT TO HIM NICELY.
NO PROBLEM, LOUIE.

1 (800) 555 - HOLY
BIG GUY
ELVIS
JFK
HOFFA
HI BIG GUY, IT'S FRED THE POSSESSED FLOWER CALLING...
... YES, I'M CALLING ON BEHALF OF MY EMPLOYER, LOUIE...
YES. IT IS REGARDING THE FAST FOOD PROMOTION...
... I'M TERRIBLY SORRY, BUT WE ARE GOING TO HAVE TO DECLINE ON YOUR REQUEST...

YOU F**K'N
A S.O.B!!
LOOK, BIG GUY. WE ARE RUNNING A BUSINESS HERE...
...OH YA! WELL YOU CAN TAKE YOUR THREATS AND BLOW THEM OUT OF YOUR DIVINE POOP SHOOT!
I LOVE YOUR SUBTLETIES...
... INSTIGATOR.
CLICK!

1985...
... HEAVEN'S BOARDROOM.
HELLO, MY EMPLOYEES.
BURNING HEDGE
JUDGE FATE
EASTER BUNNY
MIKE
MOE
SANTA
SLAM!
LOUIE AND FRED THINK THAT THEY ARE THE ONLY ONES WHO CAN PLAY HARD BALL.
THEY HAVE REFUSED TO RECALL THEIR FAST FOOD PROMOTION, LEAVING ME NO OTHER CHOICE BUT TO COUNTER ATTACK.

WE WILL RETALIATE BY INTRODUCING FITNESS CLUBS AND WAIT LOSS CENTERS INTO SOCIETY.
BY MAKING GYMS READILY AVAILABLE AND INCREASING HEALTH CONSCIENCE, WE CAN RECTIFY THE FAST FOOD DILEMMA.
100 lbs
BRILLIANT PLAN BIG GUY.
I DO BELIEVE THAT WE HAVE A WINNER.

HOLY FITNESS
SILICON VALLEY BLVD
A LITTLE BICEP CURL OVA HEIA AND A LITTLE TRICEP PULL DOWN OVA THEIA.
500lb
500lb
SKINNY FATTERSON'S WEIGHT LOSS CENTER
MAXIMUM CAPACITY 666 ZILLION TONS
I AM SO PROUD OF ALL OF YOU.
SLOBS.

SOCIETY IN GENERAL IS BECOMING HEALTHIER AND WE ARE LOSING INCOME!
HELL'S IN-STORE TRAFFIC INDEX IS DOWN BY A CONSIDERABLE PERCENT.PEOPLE ARE STARTINGTO IGNORE FAST FOOD!
I'LL HAVE A VEGGIE DOG WITH EXTRA BEAN SPROUTS, PLEASE.
AND I'LL HAVE A SLICE OF GOAT CHEESE PIZZA TOPPED WITH A BUNCH OF NON-FAT STUFF.

1996... HELL'S BOARDROOM...
AS WE ALL KNOW FAST FOOD SALES ARE DOWN DUE TO THE NEW HEALTH CRAZE.
FITNESS CLUBS AND WEIGHT LOSS CENTERS ARE PREVENTING HELL FROM REACHING A LOT OF POTENTIAL CUSTOMERS.
FAST FOOD
NATURAL CAUSES!
DISEASE
BOOZE
DRUGS
TOO MUCH
PSYCHIC CHAT LINE
AS YOU CAN SEE FROM THIS CHART, FAST FOOD CONTRIBUTES TO A SMALL PERCENTAGE OF DEATH'S OVER ALL, MARKET SHARE.

THE BIG GUY HAS IMPLEMENTED A HEALTH CRAZE TO COUNTER ACT OUR FAST FOOD PROMOTION. WHAT WE NEED IS SOMETHING THAT IS STRONG ENOUGH TO VANQUISH SOCIETIES HEALTHY MIND SET.
SO I PURPOSE THAT WE LEGALIZE DRUGS AND PROSTITUTION TO COUNTER ACT THE BIG GUY'S HEALTH CRAZE.

WHAT?

PROSTITUTION WOULD SURE MAKE MY JOB A HELL OF A LOT MORE INTERESTING.

MY HOMEBOYS CALL ME, FUNKY, DOPE, STUPID, CUPID.

DY-NO-MITE!!!

LEGALIZED DRUGS = HELL!

IT'S THE BOOGIEMAN!!!
OH NO!!!, DISCO IS BACK!
I'VE GOT THE MUNCHIES!!!
FAR OUT!
HOW THE HELL ARE YOU GONNA PULL THAT OFF, FRED?
HOW WOULD YOU EVER GET AWAY WITH INSTATING SUCH A FRIVOLOUS SET OF LAWS?

SIMPLY BY NEGOTIATING ONE HELL OF A DEAL WITH THE DEVIL.
THE BIG GUY IS DEFINITELY GOING TO HAVE A HOLY COW.

1999... THE OVAL OFFICE...
666
THE STANDARD PRESIDENTIAL CONTRACT.
THE END!

HAPPY PREDATOR PUBLICATIONS
HAPPY NICK'S
FRED THE POSSESSED FLOWER
3
IF ARMAGGEDON IS A FAT SINGER... THEN EARTH IS A GIANT FRIED PEANUT BUTTER AND BANANA SANDWICH!!!
SERIOUSLY?!
"INTERVIEW WITH A DEMON"
GUEST STARRING: GOD & SATAN

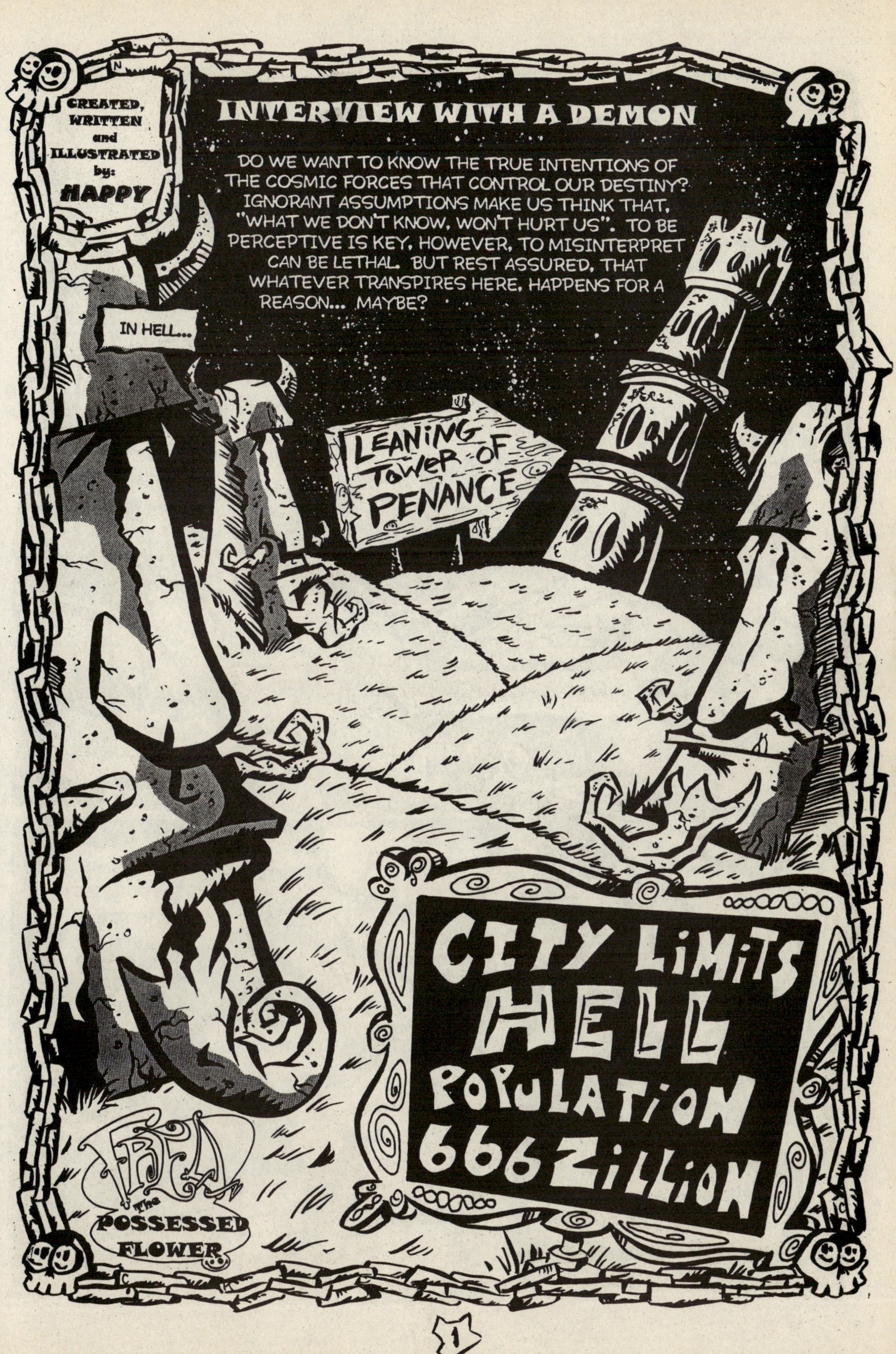
CREATED, WRITTEN and ILLUSTRATED by: HAPPY
INTERVIEW WITH A DEMON
DO WE WANT TO KNOW THE TRUE INTENTIONS OF THE COSMIC FORCES THAT CONTROL OUR DESTINY? IGNORANT ASSUMPTIONS MAKE US THINK THAT, "WHAT WE DON'T KNOW, WON'T HURT US". TO BE PERCEPTIVE IS KEY, HOWEVER, TO MISINTERPRET CAN BE LETHAL. BUT REST ASSURED, THAT WHATEVER TRANSPIRES HERE, HAPPENS FOR A REASON... MAYBE?
IN HELL...
LEANING TOWER OF PENANCE
CITY LIMITS
HELL
POPULATION
666 ZILLION
FREA The POSSESSED FLOWER

FRED'S OFFICE...
... SOMEWHERE IN HELL.
EXCUSE ME FRED, THIS IS JIMMY, THE LITTLE BOY WHO MADE AN APPOINTMENT TO INTERVIEW YOU FOR HIS SCHOOL PROJECT.
GOOD MORNING, MR. POSSESSED FLOWER.
YES, OF COURSE...
COME ON IN JIMMY... AND CALL ME FRED. BEFORE WE GET STARTED, WOULD YOU LIKE A DRINK?
PERHAPS SOME O.J., THE GUILTIEST DRINK IN TOWN!
NO THANKS.

I'D LIKE TO START OFF BY ASKING YOU, WHAT IS YOUR FAVORITE ASPECT OF BEING LOUIE'S RIGHT HAND MAN?
THAT'S AN EASY ONE...
... NEGOTIATING PERSONAL CONTRACTS WITH PEOPLE IN EXCHANGE FOR THEIR SOULS.
I THOUGHT THAT PEOPLE MADE DEALS WITH THE DEVIL, DIRECTLY.
NO WAY, HE'S MUCH TOO BUSY GARDENING, GOLFING AND PLAYING WITH HIS MODEL AIRPLANES. I RUN EVERYTHING, LOUIE SIMPLY OWNS THE PLACE.
WOULD YOU LIKE FOR ME TO SHARE SOME EXAMPLES OF PREVIOUSLY BROKEN CONTRACTS PERTAINING TO RELEVANT TURNING POINTS IN HISTORY?

TWO MILLION, BC...
BEFORE COMMERCIALISM
...THE INVENTION OF THE WHEEL.
?
ZAP!
DO YOU WANT TO PLAY...
LET'S MAKE A WHEEL?

UGH!
!

JACK HAMMER!
RTATATATATATATA!!!!
UGH?

A WHEEL LATER...
DYNO TREAD WHEELS
UGH
UGH?
UGH...
UGH...
UGH?
UGH!

POP!
TIME TO COLLECT!
UHG!
GREEDY, EH?
AHHHH!
UGH @!!$*&!!
RIGHT THEN AND THERE I KNEW THAT MANKIND WAS GOING TO BE FUN TO DEAL WITH.

THE FALL OF ATLANTIS...
ATLANTIS WAS IN THE FURTHEST DEPTHS OF THE OCEAN, WHERE IT GETS QUITE DARK & COLD. POSEIDON, THEIR LEADER SOLD HIS SOUL TO ME SO THAT I WOULD COVER ATLANTIS' HYDRO TAB.
HYDRO TAB?
YOU CAN IMAGINE THE SIZE OF THEIR BILL.

I'M HERE TO COLLECT
I DON'T THINK SO. I AM THE MOST POWERFUL RULER OF THE MOST POWERFUL KINGDOM...
...YOU CAN'T DO ANYTHING TO ME!
SERIOUSLY?
POSEIDON WOULDN'T CO-OPERATE SO...
SO WHAT DID YOU DO TO HIM?
LET ME ANSWER THAT QUESTION WITH A QUESTION...
...CAN ANYBODY EVEN FIND ATLANTIS NOW?

1944... GERMANY...
QVICK, BREAK OUT ZA POOPA SCOOPA, I'M IN DEEP VON KA KA!!!
LOOK ADOLF, IF YOU HAD SHAVED OFF THAT RIDICULOUS LOOKING MUSTACHE BY THE DATE SPECIFIED IN OUR CONTRACT, I WOULDN'T HAVE HAD TO THROW THAT LITTLE RUSSIAN THING YOUR WAY.
I HAVE NEVER SEEN ANYTHING SO PITIFUL SINCE JONI LOVED CHACHI.
ARE THERE ANY CONTRACTS THAT HAVE YET TO BE BROKEN?
SURE THEY'RE ARE A LOT OF PRESENTLY LUCRATIVE CONTRACTS. THE BEAUTIFUL THING IS THAT IT REALLY DOESN'T MATTER IF A CONTRACT IS BROKEN OR FULFILLED BECAUSE AT THE END OF IT ALL... THEY BELONG TO ME.

FOR EXAMPLE, THE OIL COMPANIES, ACTORS, MUSICIANS, ATHLETES. THE GUY THAT INVENTED FAKE BOOBS.
NOT TO MENTION EVERY LAST POLITICIAN ON THE FACE OF THE PLANET.
WHO WOULD YOU SAY HAS RECEIVED THE BEST DEAL FROM YOU?
I WOULD HAVE TO SAY THE PLAY GUY, WITH THE MAGAZINES AND THAT TALL GUY WHO USED TO RIDE IN HIS CAR AT NIGHT AND THEN DECIDED TO BECOME A LIFEGUARD SO HE COULD WATCH THE BAY.
KIT CAR

JIMMY, IN THIS TYPE OF BUSINESS IT IS VERY EASY TO GET SIDE TRACKED.
FOR EXAMPLE, THE TIME I WENT TO HOLLYWOOD TO OFFER A STRUGGLING ACTOR A DEAL WITH THE DEVIL. BEFORE I HAD A CHANCE TO LAND THE CONTRACT...
I MET A FAST TALKING HOLLYWOOD AGENT...
THE NAME IS MR. YOUOFF, BUT YOU CAN CALL ME, RIP!
WITH YOUR UNIQUE LOOK AND MY SHIFTINESS, I COULD MAKE YOU A STAR. JUST THINK OF ALL OF THE CELEBS YOU COULD MINGLE WITH. JUST THINK OF ALL OF THE GLAMOUR AND FAME!
BUT...
...AS YOUR PERSONAL REPRESENTATIVE, I WILL REQUIRE 75%, TO START.
SERIOUSLY?

YOU'RE STEALING MY OPPORTUNITY! I HATE YOU!!!
DO YOU KNOW WHAT ACTOR HELL IS?
NO?
POP!

I THINK I'LL HAVE THE LOBSTER WITH RICE. BUT COULD YOU PUT JUST A SQUIRT OF LEMON ON THE LOBSTER. AND OH, I KNOW, COULD YOU REALLY FLUFF UP THE RICE. BUT DON'T OVER FLUFF IT.
THAT SOUNDS DIVINE. MAKE THAT TWO. BUT COULD YOU PUT A COUPLE OF SQUIRTS OF LEMON ON THE LOBSTER AND ONLY FLUFF UP MY RICE A BIT. THANKS SO MUCH, DARLING.
WILL THAT BE EVERYTHING?
OF COURSE NOT...
WHAT DO YOU HAVE ON YOUR WINE LIST, IN ALPHABETICAL ORDER?

MY BIG BREAK...
I HAVE GOT TO FIND A FRESH, NEW, VILLAIN FOR YOU TO FACE IN THE NEXT PERMINATOR MOVIE.
DIRE
HOW ABOUT...
... THE PERMINATOR VS. FRED THE POSSESSED FLOWER?!
YOU WANT ME TO FIGHT A STUPID LITTLE FLOWA?
WHAT COULD IT HURT, GIRLY MAN?
BLAM!!!

YOU'RE HIRED!
SOMEBODY GET THIS FLOWER TO WARDROBE.
WHAAA?!!!

FREDDY GOES TO...
HOLLYWOOD

FRED the POSSESSED FLOWER
MY DRESSING ROOM...

I COULD GET USED TO THIS!
POLLINATION TO THE LEFT OF ME,
POLLINATION TO THE RIGHT OF ME!

AT THE SPELLING MANSION...
OR MAYBE IT WAS THE OPRAH MANSION... OR JUST SOME PISH, POSH PARTY PAD...
WHERE EVER, WHO CARES?
YOU ARE LIKE SO WEIRD.
MUST TRY TO MAKE CONTACT WITH SENTIENT, BOTANICAL, LIFE FORM... MISTER.
THERE WERE ALWAYS SOULS FOR SALE AT THE HOLLYWOOD PARTIES.
HEY, FRED, LONG TIME NO SEE!
DIVINE INTERVENTION, MY ASS!
HEY HUE, DID YOU DO A BAD THING?

BACK AT THE OFFICE...
IT WAS FUN FOR AWHILE. BUT I REALIZED THAT MY PLACE WAS WITH LOUIE, HERE IN HELL.
AS FAR AS MY MOVIE CAREER WAS CONCERNED... IT WAS ANCIENT HISTORY.
HEY, PERMINATOR, JUST RELAX FOR A SECOND. HOW WOULD YOU LIKE TO MAKE A DEAL?
I DON'T MAKE DEALS WITH STUPID LITTLE FLOWAS.
HEY, BOBBY, I MEAN LOUIE, DID HE JUST INSULT ME?
JUST A LITTLE BIT. JUST A LITTLE BIT.
THAT'S IT! SOMEBODY GIVE ME A PENCIL SO THAT I CAN SIGN MY JOHN HANCOCK INTO HIS FREAKIN' NECK!!!

... SOMEWHERE IN HELL.
IT'S TOO BAD ABOUT THAT STRUGGLING ACTOR IMPALING HIMSELF WITH A SET OF COMPLEMENTARY CHOPSTICKS BEFORE I HAD A CHANCE TO RE-OFFER HIM A CONTRACT.

WHAT ELSE DO YOU DO DOWN HERE, IN HELL?
FRED'S OFFICE... IN HELL....
DEVIL'S ADVOCATE
FRED, THE EVIL, MARKETING GENIUS
I AM IN CHARGE OF HELL'S NEW PRODUCTS AND PROMOTIONS. I WAS RESPONSIBLE FOR FAST FOOD, FOSSIL FUEL AND YOKO OH-NO. IT WAS ALL FRONT PAGE MATERIAL IN HELL'S DAILY NEWSPAPER, THE DEVIL'S ADVOCATE.
DID YOU HAVE ANY HAND IN CREATING SEXISM, RACISM OR ANY ABUSE TOWARDS CHILDREN OR ANIMALS AND SO FORTH?
HERE IN HELL WE THINK OF INTELLIGENT PROMOTIONS TO INCREASE CLIENTELE AND GENERATE REVENUE. BUT TO ANSWER YOUR QUESTION...
NO, I HAD NOTHING TO DO WITH THAT. THOSE ARE ALL PRODUCTS OF OUR BIGGEST SUPPLIER, HUMANITY INC...
TWISTED, AREN'T THEY?
HAVE YOU EVER RECALLED ANY PRODUCTS?
UMM?
THERE HAS BEEN THE ODD PROMOTION THAT I HAVE HAD TO RECALL...

... LIKE THE TIME THAT KIDS UNANIMOUSLY DECIDED THAT THEY DIDN'T WANT TO LISTEN TO THEIR PARENTS ANYMORE.
WE, THE CHILDREN OF THE PLANET, WILL ENDORSE AND ADVERTISE THE DEVIL IN THE FORM OF VARIOUS MERCHANDISE, MUSIC AND TV. IN RETURN WE WANT TO EAT WHAT WE WANT, GO TO BED WHEN WE WANT AND DO WHAT EVER WE WANT.
WE ALSO WANT IMMUNITY FROM BEING GROUNDED AND OR HAVING TO DO HOMEWORK.
AT FIRST I THOUGHT IT WOULD BE A GOOD IDEA BECAUSE THE KIDS WOULD BURN THEMSELVES OUT INTO GUT ROTTED, VIDEO GAME PLAYING, MINDLESS, FUN JUNKIES.
BUT THEN...

ALL OF THE PARENTS WERE WORRYING AND MISERABLE. BUT THEN THEY ALL STARTED PRAYING FOR THE KID'S, WHICH PUT THEM IN THE BIG GUY'S GOOD BOOK AND OFF OF MY POTENTIAL CLIENT LIST.
NOW THAT'S WHAT I LIKE TO SEE.
THE KIDS WENT THE ROUTE THAT I HAD ANTICIPATED. THEN SOMETHING HAPPENED THAT I DIDN'T COUNT ON...
... DRINKING TOILET CLEANER...
... TEASING BIG DOGS...
GRRRR!
TWEEK!
... DRIVING THEIR PARENTS CARS...
CRASH!
AND SO FORTH.

KIDS STARTED CROAKING LEFT, RIGHT AND CENTER. I REALIZED THAT IF THIS KEPT UP, THE HUMAN RACE WOULD BECOME EXTINCT.
IF THAT HAPPENED I WOULDN'T HAVE ANY MORE CUSTOMERS AND HELL WOULD EVENTUALLY GO OUT OF BUSINESS. SO YOU CAN SEE THAT I HAD TO CANCEL THAT PROMOTION IN ORDER TO KEEP A STEADY AND CONTINUOUS CUSTOMER FLOW.
RIP

ANOTHER PROMOTION THAT I HAD IMPLEMENTED AND THEN RECALLED WAS THE CONCEPT OF ROBOT SLAVES.
THE IDEA BEHIND THIS WAS TO LET PEOPLE GET LAZY AND OUT OF SHAPE SO THAT THEY WOULDN'T LIVE AS LONG. IN TURN, HELL WOULD RECEIVE MORE CLIENTS.
INSTEAD PEOPLE BECAME ENERGETIC AND HAPPY, FULFILLING ALL OF THE DREAMS AND GOALS THEY PREVIOUSLY COULDN'T ATTAIN.
PEOPLE HAD NOTHING BETTER TO DO THAN BE NICE TO THEIR FELLOW MAN. POVERTY, DISEASE, PREJUDICE, SEXISM AND CRIME WERE ERADICATED.
GOOD MORNING. HOW'S THAT VINTAGE CAR COLLECTION OF YOURS COMING?
HOW ARE YOU DOING? ARE YOU STILL WORKING ON THAT GIANT SCULPTURE?
BEAUTIFUL DAY, ISN'T IT? I THINK THAT I'M GOING TO GO DEEP-SEA DIVING.
SO NOT ONLY DID PEOPLE PHYSICALLY LIVE LONGER, BUT THE MAJORITY OF THEM WENT TO HEAVEN DUE TO THEIR NEW FOUND HUMANITY. ... PITY.

60+
60+
60+
OVER THE HILL
GEEZER
#1 GRANNY

THE MOST ANNOYING PROMOTION THAT I EVER IMPLEMENTED AND THEN HAD TO RECALL WAS A LAW THAT STATED EVERYONE OVER 60 YEARS OLD WAS TO UNDERGO EUTHANASIA TO HELP EARTH'S POPULATION CONTROL PROBLEM.

IN HELL...

HERE IS MY SENIOR CITIZENS CARD, SONNY.

THIS WOULD INCREASE HELLS IN-STORE TRAFFIC. BUT, THE PROBLEM WAS THAT WITH ALL OF THE SENIOR CITIZEN DISCOUNTS, EVERYONE OVER 60 YEARS OF AGE, WAS RECEIVING THE LOWEST RATES ON HEAVENLY REDEMPTION.

THEY WERE ALSO CHEAP TIPPERS...

HERE YOU GO YOU LITTLE WHIPPERSNAPPER. DON'T SPEND IT ALL IN ONE PLACE.

WE WEREN'T MAKING ENOUGH PROFIT TO COVER OUR MANPOWER AND EXPENSES, SO WE RECALLED THE PROMOTION AND TOOK A LOSS.

ALL DEDUCTIBLE, OF COURSE.

DO YOU CURRENTLY HAVE ANYTHING ON THE DRAWING BOARD?
BUT OF COURSE! HERE IS A SNEAK PEAK AT SOME OF THE CHAOTIC FESTIVITIES THAT I HAVE PLANNED FOR THE TURN OF THE CENTURY...
I SAY WE ATTACK NOW! BEFORE MAN REALIZES THAT WE CAN SPEAK!

YOU REMEMBER US DON'T YOU...
MR. ASSORTED SPRINKLES AND MR. CHOCOLATE GLAZE?

RIGHT COME BACK,
WRONG KING!
HAIL KING!

I DON'T WANT TO GIVE TOO MUCH AWAY...
BUT I WILL LEAVE YOU WITH ONE LAST HINT FOR THINGS TO COME.
WHAT WORD STARTS WITH THE LETTER B AND RHYMES WITH MOM?
HA HA
HA HA
HA HA
HA HA
HA HA
HA HA
HA HA
THE END!

HAPPY PREDATOR PUBLICATIONS
FRED the POSSESSED FLOWER
4
by: HAPPY NICK
"THE PEOPLE VS HELL"
GUEST STARRING: GOD & SATAN

THE PEOPLE VS. HELL
EVEN THE MIGHTIEST OF PEOPLE CAN BE MANIPULATED FOR BETTER OR WORSE. THE POWERS THAT BE CAN CAGE AND OR RELEASE ANYONE, AT ANYTIME. ADAPTING TO A SITUATION IS POSSIBLE BY ANALYZING OPTIONS IN A LOGICAL AND UNOBSTRUCTED WAY. TO UTILIZE YOUR STRENGTHS YOU MUST BE AWARE OF YOUR WEAKNESSES. PRETTY DEEP... EH?
HELL
STATUE OF PERGATORY
CREATED, WRITTEN and ILLUSTRATED by: HAPPY
EDEN'S BIG APPLE
the POSSESSED FLOWER

FRED'S OFFICE... IN HELL....
LOOK MOTHER NATURE, FOR THE LAST TIME...
IF YOU DON'T LET MAN, HUNT WHALES TO EXTINCTION, I'M GOING TO LOSE ALL OF THOSE WHALING FISHERMEN AS GUARANTEED CUSTOMERS! HELP ME OUT HERE BABY.
CLICK!
HELLO? HELLO?
I GUESS THAT SHE IS ONE OF THOSE, "DON'T CALL ME A CHICK", CHICKS.
EXCUSE ME, FRED. BUT MICHEAL IS HERE TO DELIVER A MESSAGE FROM THE BIG GUY. HE DOESN'T HAVE AN APPOINTMENT.
THAT'S OK, GRETCHEN.
LET HIM IN.
A-C

WHAT CAN I DO FOR YOU, MIKE?
THE BIG GUY WOULD LIKE TO HAVE A MEETING WITH YOU, ASAP.
THE BIG GUY ALWAYS DEALS WITH LOUIE ONE ON ONE. WANT DOES HE WANT WITH ME?
I'M JUST THE MESSENGER, FRED.
YA... YOU KNOW WHAT ALWAYS HAPPENS TO THE MESSENGER... MIKE?
FRED THE POSSESSED FLOWER OFFICE
KABOOM!!!

COCKY, WINGED WEENIE. I DON'T HAVE ANYTHING TO BE NERVOUS ABOUT. IT'S JUST A MEETING.
THE PEARLY GATES...
BING!
WWWWHHHYYYYY ARE YOU HERE, BIG BOSS? TO SEE THE BIG GUY?
GO FLY A KITE, HE SAYS.
I ADMIT IT... I FOOLED PEOPLE INTO BELIEVING THAT MY STUFF WAS GOOD.
BUT PLEASE, LET ME STAY UP HERE.
HEY MAN, THANKS FOR THE QUALITY SH...
I'M NOT IN THE MOOD, OK?

THE BIG GUY IS EXPECTING YOU.
HEY, BURNING HEDGE, CAN YOU TELL ME WHERE I CAN FIND HEAVEN'S MINISTRY OF FIRE CODES AND SAFETY STANDARDS?
VERY FUNNY.
HELLO, BIG GUY.
YOU WANTED TO SEE ME?

I'LL GET RIGHT TO THE POINT, FRED. I KNOW THAT YOU ARE A BUSY FLOWER. YOU ARE CONSTANTLY DOING EVIL THINGS ON HELL'S BEHALF...
NEGOTIATING DEALS FOR THE DEVIL...
IMPLEMENTING SINFUL PROMOTIONS TO INCREASE HELL'S CUSTOMER BASE AND MOST OF ALL...
...MAKING THINGS DIFFICULT FOR ME AND MY STAFF!
THAT'S VERY PERCEPTIVE, BIG GUY. BUT WHAT IS YOUR POINT?
I WANT YOU TO STOP WORKING FOR LOUIE AND START PUTTING YOUR TALENTS TO POSITIVE USE.
SERIOUSLY?
WELL BIG GUY, I DON'T THINK THAT YOU SEE THE GARDEN THROUGH THE FLOWERS. SO...
I AM GOING TO HAVE TO POLITELY DECLINE.

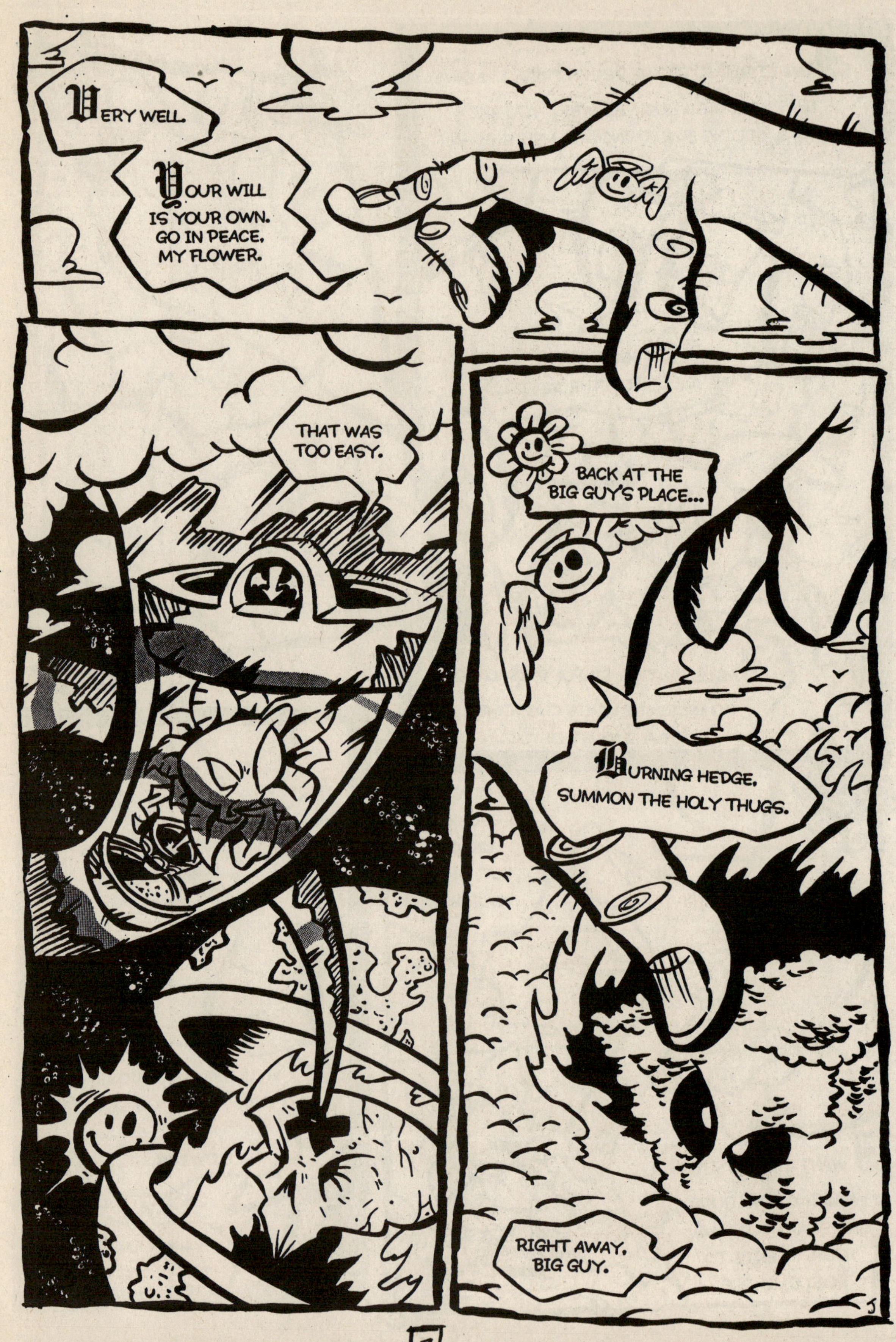
VERY WELL.
YOUR WILL IS YOUR OWN. GO IN PEACE, MY FLOWER.
THAT WAS TOO EASY.
BACK AT THE BIG GUY'S PLACE...
BURNING HEDGE. SUMMON THE HOLY THUGS.
RIGHT AWAY, BIG GUY.

FRED'S OFFICE...
I DON'T THINK THAT YOU REALIZE HOW BADLY YOUR COMPANY NEEDS A DEAL WITH THE DEVIL, MR. HELLMARK.
WHY? YOU ASK...
HELL #1
BECAUSE NOTHING SAYS, A FLAGRANT WAIST OF PRECIOUS WOODLANDS, THEN A GREETING CARD!
HAPPY BITE ME!!!
HAPPY GET A NOSE JOB!
HAPPY SUCKS!!
HAPPY LOSE SOME WEIGHT!
HAPPY THANX FOR NOTHIN'!!!
?!

CRASH!!!
WHAT THE HEAVEN?!

ANGELIC ASSASSINS ARE SO TASTY.

GULP!!!

ARGGG!!!

GAAK!!!

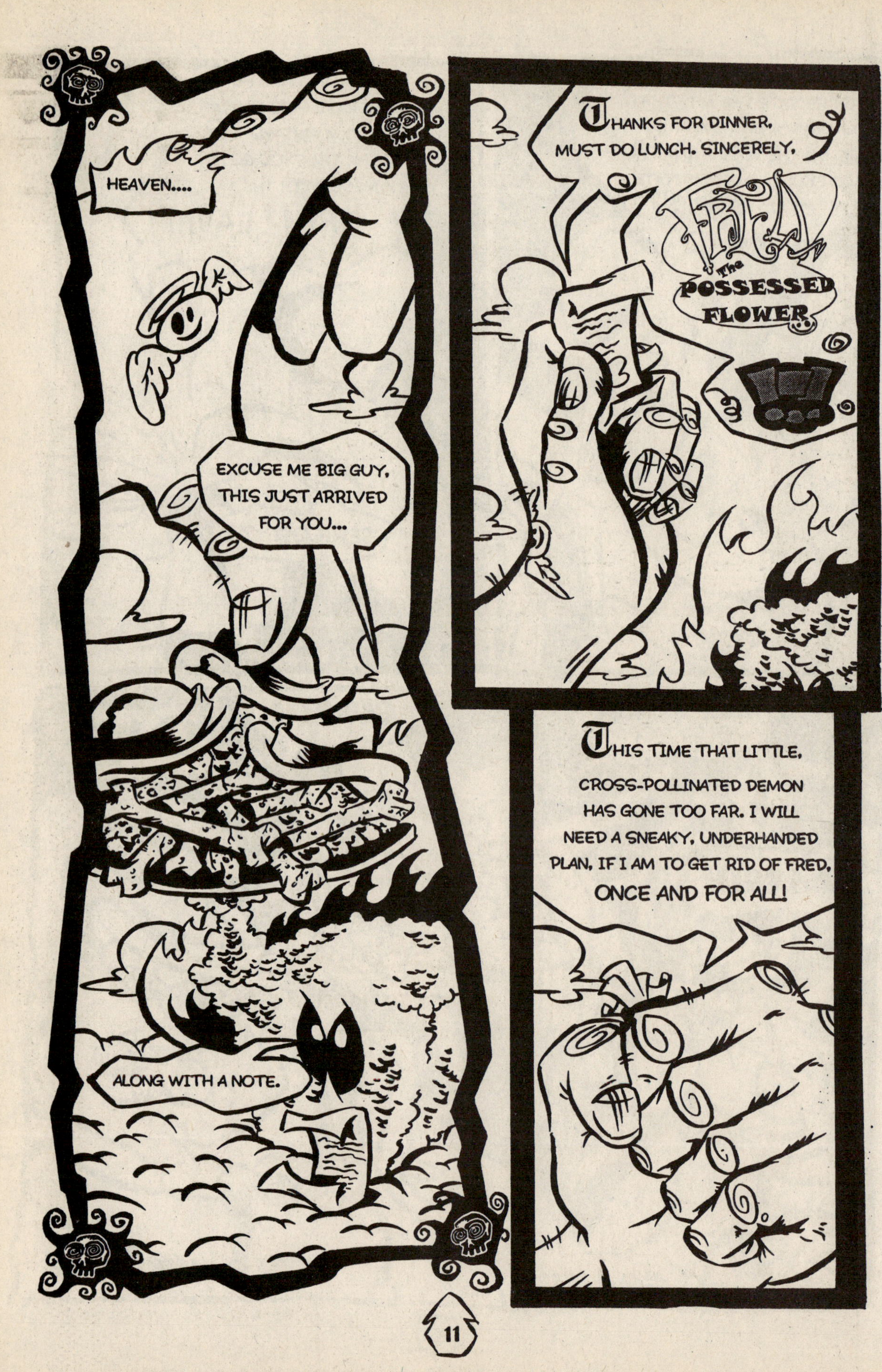
HEAVEN....
EXCUSE ME BIG GUY, THIS JUST ARRIVED FOR YOU...
ALONG WITH A NOTE.
THANKS FOR DINNER, MUST DO LUNCH. SINCERELY,
FRED The POSSESSED FLOWER
THIS TIME THAT LITTLE, CROSS-POLLINATED DEMON HAS GONE TOO FAR. I WILL NEED A SNEAKY, UNDERHANDED PLAN, IF I AM TO GET RID OF FRED, ONCE AND FOR ALL!

HOWDY?
WHAT IF YOU SENT RUDOLF THE UGLY FACED ANGEL TO INFILTRATE HELL AS AN INDUSTRIAL SPY. THEN ALL OF THE OTHER ANGELS WILL LOVE HIM AND LET HIM JOIN IN ALL OF THEIR ANGEL GAMES.
GOOD THINKING, BURNING HEDGE. I COULDN'T HAVE SAID IT BETTER, MYSELF.
BY DECREASING LOUIE AND FRED'S CREDIBILITY, I WILL INCREASE RUDOLF'S POPULARITY. THEN I CAN KILL TWO PREVERBAL BIRDS WITH ONE HOLY STONE. DAMN, I'M GOOD!
...OOPS, I'LL SAY TEN HALE LARRY'S AND FORGIVE MYSELF LATER.
I WANT YOU TO DIG UP SOME DIRT ON FRED THE POSSESSED FLOWER. THE DARKER THE SOIL, THE BETTER!

A DEMONIC HEALTH SPA...
... SOMEWHERE IN HELL.
LEAF MANICURE, MR. POSSESSED FLOWER?
CLICK!
REC
HI, THIS IS FRED THE POSSESSED FLOWER CALLING. MAY I PLEASE SPEAK WITH PURGATORY'S VP OF MARKETING?
THIS IS THE BOOGIE MAN SPEAKING, HOW CAN I HELP YOU?
HEY! BOOGIE MAN, IT'S FRED...
I NEED A FAVOR...
CAN YOU PUT A FALSE MARK-UP ON THE BABY BOOMER- SOUL SAVER RATES. THAT WAY I CAN HOLD A SALE AND TRICK THE CUSTOMERS INTO PAYING AS MUCH, IF NOT MORE THAN BEFORE.
NO PROBLEM, BROTHER.
THANKS, BOOGIEMAN. SO, HOW'S EVERYTHING GOING AT THE NEW JOB?

SOIL CHANGE, MR. POSSESSED FLOWER?

INCRIMINATING, WOULDN'T YOU SAY?

REC

FRED'S OFFICE...

STAFF

I KNOW THAT YOU ARE SMUGGLING ILLEGAL CHOCOLATE EASTER EGGS INTO SOCIETY, FROM A CHEAP LABOR FACTORY IN SOUTH AMERICA.

REC

HUH!!!

COME ON FRED, GIVE ME A BREAK. I'M JUST TRYING TO SURVIVE LIKE THE NEXT GUY. IF THE BIG GUY FINDS OUT...
...HE'LL REPLACE ME BEFORE I CAN WIGGLE BY CUTE LITTLE NOSE...
...AND THEN HE'LL SKIN MY FUZZY ASS AND TURN ME INTO A HARP, OR SOMETHING!
SERIOUSLY? WELL, MR. EASTER BUNNY...
I'LL TELL YOU WHAT I'LL DO. IF YOU SIGN YOUR SOUL OVER TO ME, I'LL ALLOW YOU TO CONTINUE THIS LITTLE, ILLEGAL CHOCOLATE SCAM... AND I PROMISE THAT THE BIG GUY WILL NEVER KNOW WHAT YOU'RE UP TO. CROSS MY STEM AND HOPE TO WILT.

EVIL TOWER
HELL
OPEN 24/7
MARKETING FRAUD AND BLACKMAIL...
THAT SHOULD DO IT. TIME TO INFORM THE BIG GUY.

LOUIE'S LIVING ROOM...

PASS THE CHEEZOS.

READ'EM AND WEEP, BOYS... EVIL FLUSH.

SMASH!

EVERYBODY FREEZE, WE'RE
THE FATE DEPARTMENT!

WHAT THE HELL'S GOING ON HERE!
FRED THE POSSESSED FLOWER. YOU ARE UNDER ARREST FOR MARKETING FRAUD AND BLACKMAIL. ANYTHING YOU SAY CAN AND WILL BE USED AGAINST YOU IN A COURT OF FATE.
THIS IS RIDICULOUS!

WE ARE CONDUCTING A FULL INTERNAL INVESTIGATION. YOU AND THE COMPANY KNOWN AS HELL ARE SCHEDULED TO BE AUDITED.
ON WHO'S AUTHORITY?!...
...AND THIS HAD BETTER BE GOOD!
THIS BUST WAS HEADED UP BY THE BIG GUY HIMSELF.
THAT'S... PRETTY GOOD.
LOUIE, HERE ARE YOUR OFFICIAL AUDIT FORMS WHICH YOU ARE REQUIRED TO FILL OUT.
HELL WILL FREEZE OVER BEFORE I AM AUDITED...
WHY IS IT SO DAMN COLD IN HERE?

FATES COURTROOM...
... SOMEWHERE IN PURGATORY.
ALL RISE FOR THE HONORABLE, JUDGE FATE.
BRING OUT THE PRISONER.
GRRR!
SPOOKY, LITTLE CARE PACKAGE.

IF IT PLEASES THE COURT, YOUR HONOR. I WOULD LIKE TO SAY A FEW WORDS.
MY CLIENT WAS APPROACHED AND GIVEN AN ULTIMATUM ABOUT HIS JOB JUST DAYS BEFORE THIS WHOLE, SORTED AFFAIR TRANSPIRED. YOUR HONOR, I CRY CORPORATE ESPIONAGE!
FOUL PLAY HAS CONVENIENTLY REARED ITS UGLY FACE... AND ITS NAME IS THE BIG GUY!
BLASPHEMY !!!

BIG GUY'S TOP 10

WHAT?

LOUIE, YOU SHOULD BE THANKFUL. IF IT WASN'T FOR THE BELL CURVE ON FATE, I WOULD HAVE ERASED YOUR EXISTENCE ON DAY ONE.
IT WAS THE FLOWER IN THE OFFICE, WITH THE CANDLESTICK!
GAAK!!!
I MEAN THE TELEPHONE!

FRED The POSSESSED FLOWER
FOR THE CHARGES OF MARKETING FRAUD, BLACKMAIL, AND NOW, DEFAMATION OF CHARACTER AND SLANDER...
I FIND YOU...
GUILTY!
THERE'S A SHOCK.
I ALSO FIND YOU IN CONTEMPT! YOU ARE HERE BY SENTENCED TO THIRTY BILLION HOURS OF COMMUNITY SERVICE...
...IN THE REINCARNATION WING OF THE FATE DEPARTMENT. THIS COURT IS ADJOURNED.
CRACK!

THE REINCARNATION WING...
...SOMEWHERE IN THE FATE DEPARTMENT.
FOR EVERY GOOD HEARTED DEED THAT YOU DO, YOU WILL BE REINCARNATED INTO A DIFFERENT FORM...
EACH CLOSER TO YOUR OWN TRUE SELF.
GREAT, MOE.
THE CITY...
WHAT IS THAT SMELL? IT'S A CROSS-BETWEEN BANANA BREAD AND FORMALDEHYDE.
OH MY GOODNESS GRACIOUSNESS. I AM LOST; NOW I WILL NEVER SEE MY FAMILY AGAIN.
TAXI
LEFT, LEFT, GO LEFT!
MAYBE I SHOULD GO LEFT.

HOLY SHITZU! THIS TIME, THEY HAVE GONE TOO FARE.
YES, OPERATOR, I'D LIKE TO MAKE A COLLECT CALL TO HELL, PLEASE.
GASP!
RING
RING
RING
RING
RING
RING

HELL'S KITCHEN...
RING!
RING
RING!
PLEASE LET THAT BE SOME SORT OF ANIMAL ACTIVIST!
HELLO...
YES, HE IS JUST HANGING OUT WITH ME...
JUST A SECOND. ...IT'S FOR YOU.

LISTEN TO ME, EASTER BUNNY...
...I HAVE A PROPOSITION FOR YOU. WE WILL MAKE A TRADE. YOUR FREEDOM, FOR MINE.
IS THIS A TRICK?
SILLY RABBIT, TRICKS ARE FOR SINNERS. SINCE YOU WORK FOR THE BIG GUY, YOU HAVE ACCESS TO ALL OF HEAVEN'S FATE FILES. I WANT YOU TO SNEAK INTO THE FATE DEPARTMENT AND ALTER MY RECORD TO SAY THAT I AM INNOCENT. IN RETURN I WILL GIVE YOU A "GET OUT OF HELL FREE" CARD. AND I WILL ALSO LET YOU OUT OF YOUR CONTRACT WITH ME, CONCERNING YOUR ILLEGAL, CHOCOLATE, IMPORTING SCAM.
WHAT IF I GET CAUGHT BREAKING INTO THE FATE DEPARTMENT?
THAT'S TOUGH RABBIT PELLETS!

SOMEWHERE TROPICAL....
HERE'S TO TEAMWORK. WE RIPPED OFF HEAVEN, AND WE RIPPED OFF HELL. WE ARE SO GOOD, AND YET SO BAD.
THIS IS WHAT HAPPENS WHEN I SCRATCH YOUR BACK AND YOU WATER MINE.

CHEERS!!!
CLANG!
THE END!

HAPPY PREDATOR PUBLICATIONS

Mooo...

HAPPY NICK'S

FRED the POSSESSED FLOWER

"TO HAVE AND TO SCOLD"

GUEST STARRING: GOD & SATAN

FREA
The POSSESSED FLOWER
TO HAVE AND TO SCOLD
LOVE IS A PURE FORM OF ENERGY THAT IS EASILY TAINTED. IT CAN MAKE SOMEONE INVINCIBLE OR CRUSH HIM OR HER INTO OBLIVION. THIS IS AN EMOTION THAT CAN CLOUD THE SMARTEST MIND OR MAKE AN IDIOT SEE CRYSTAL CLEAR. BUT THEN AGAIN... WHAT'S LOVE GOT TO DO WITH IT?
CREATED, WRITTEN and ILLUSTRATED by: HAPPY
IN LIMBO...
HOLYMPICS

GOOD AFTERNOON LADIES AND GENTLEMEN...
AND WELCOME BACK TO HEAVEN, WHERE WE ARE HOSTING THE 666TH SUPERNATURAL
HOLYMPIC GAMES.
I'M YOUR COMMENTATOR, JUDGE FATE OF THE FATE DEPARTMENT AND THIS IS MY HOLY CO-HOST, THE BURNING HEDGE.
INTRODUCING THE THREE LEADING TEAMS...
LEADING IN FIRST PLACE, THE DEMONS AND THEIR COACH, FRED THE POSSESSED FLOWER.
MENTAL NOTE, FEAR IS AN EXCELLENT MOTIVATIONAL TOOL.

WE'RE GONNA FRY THOSE FREAKY DOO DEMONS LIKE A BUNCH OF PEANUT BUTTER AND BANANA SANDWICHES.
FOLLOWING CLOSELY IN SECOND PLACE ARE THE FAMOUS, DEAD GUYS WITH THEIR COACH, MR. ROBINSON.
LET'S SPLIT UP AND ATTACK NOW, WHILE THEY ARE UNSUSPECTING!
AND FINALLY IN THIRD PLACE IS THE HOME TEAM. THE ANGELS AND THEIR COACH, ADAM.
CENSORED
NOW REMEMBER TEAM, DON'T BE TEMPTED TO GO FOR THE GLORY. GLORY IS AN AGGRESSIVELY BASED STATE OF MIND.

IN THE STANDS...
#1
HEY MOE, I'LL BET YOU THAT MY GUYS WILL TAKE FIRST PLACE.
THY SHALL NOT BET ON THOU FELLOW MAN. DID THY, THOU, THOUGH SAY THAT CORRECTLY?
WHATEVER.
SO WHAT ABOUT YOU BIG GUY? ARE YOU UP FOR SOME ACTION?
LOUIE, WHY DON'T YOU BEHAVE AND GRAB US A COUPLE OF HOTDOGS.

OK FOLKS, TIME FOR THE FINAL EVENT TO SEE WHICH TEAM WILL GO HOME WITH THE MOST GOLDS.
WELL JUDGE FATE, I THINK THAT FREUD IS REALLY GOING TO HAVE TO USE HIS HEAD IN THIS EVENT IF HE IS TO BE VICTORIOUS.
KEEP YOUR GUARD UP!
TELL ME ABOUT YOUR MOTHER.
BAM!
THE WINNER!

WE WON!!!
HEY MOE, NEXT YEAR WE'RE GONNA PUT THE FIX ON... I'M GETTING SICK OF FRED'S TEAM ALWAYS WINNING.
WHATEVER YOU SAY, BIG GUY.
#1
#1

THE NEXT DAY IN LOUIE'S BACKYARD...
YOU WANTED TO SEE ME, LOUIE?
I JUST WANTED TO CONGRATULATE YOU ON YOUR SUPERB JOB OF COACHING THE HOLYMPIC DEMON TEAM.
I ALSO WANTED TO TELL YOU THAT YOU ARE DOING A GREAT JOB AT WORK.
HEY, FRED...
WHAT I'M TRYING TO SAY, IS THAT YOU DESERVE A VACATION. I HOPE THAT YOU CAN PRY YOURSELF AWAY FRO...
WHERE DID YOU GO?

THE OFFICE...
EVERYTHING IS UNPLUGGED AND MY RESERVATIONS ARE IN ORDER. I DON'T THINK THAT I AM FORGETTING ANYTHING.
INCASE OF A PROBLEM, YOU HAVE ALL OF MY REACHABLE NUMBERS.
YES SIR. HAVE A GOOD TIME, SIR.

ON A PLANE...
HEADED SOMEWHERE TROPICAL...
CAN I GET YOU A BEVERAGE, OR PERHAPS SOME FRESH SOIL FOR YOUR POT, SIR?
AIR HELL
LOUIE'S BACKYARD...
CUPID, I NEED YOU TO DO ME A FAVOR.
NAME IT, LOUIE.
AS YOU KNOW, FRED HAS JUST GONE ON VACATION. WHAT I WOULD LIKE IS FOR YOU TO SECRETLY ARRANGE FOR FRED TO FIND A COMPANION.
CONSIDER IT DONE.

PARADISE...
ZZZZZZZ
HMMM?
ZING!!!
AUSTA LA VISTA,
FREDDY!

BOING!
WHAT'S YOUR NAME, SHORT, DARK AND OMNIVOROUS?
I'M GINGER.
MY NAME IS FRED THE PERVERTED FL...
I MEAN FRED THE POSSESSED FLOWER.
CUTESY STUFF... YUCK!

FRIED GREEN MONGOLIAN
MENU
OUR FINEST WATER, MISEUR POSSESSED FLOWER.

I'LL HAVE A DOUBLE SCOOP OF INNER DEMON SHERBERT, WITH SOME CRUSHED SPIRIT SPRINKLED ON TOP.

SINGING IN THE PAIN!, WHAT A GLORIOUS FEELING, I'M SATANISTIC AGAIN!!!
FRED AND GINGER WERE ALWAYS MEANT TO DO THIS NUMBER.
I NEVER THOUGHT THAT I WOULD ENJOY DOING MUSHY THINGS.

SHE LOVES ME...
SHE LOVES ME NOT.
TWEEK!
FRED, DO YOU TAKE THIS WOMAN TO BE YOUR LAWFUL WEDDED WIFE?
I DO.
POLLINATE UNTIL YOUR EYES POP OUT!
GINGER, DO YOU TAKE THIS FLOWER TO BE YOUR LAWFUL WEDDED HUSBAND?

MONTHS DOWN
THE ROAD.
AT FRED'S PRIVATE
SOLARIUM...
MOMMA!
MOMMA!
WAY TO GO, DADDIO.

HOME SWEET HOME
PARADISE?
GINGER, WHAT'S FOR DINNER? HONEY?
WHEN WAS THE LAST TIME YOU TOOK ME OUT FOR DINNER?
ALL YOU EVER DO ANYMORE IS WATCH TV! YOU DON'T PAY ANY ATTENTION TO ME ANY MORE....
DID YOU EVEN HEAR ME?
...DID YOU?
...FRED?
WHAT?
WHY CAN'T YOU BE MORE SENSITIVE, CARING OR ATTENTIVE. YOU DON'T EVEN KNOW HOW TO BOIL WATER...
AND CONVENIENTLY, YOU STILL DON'T EVEN KNOW WHERE THE VACUUM IS!

HEY, DAD, I'M GONNA HOT WIRE YOUR CAR AND BE BACK AT AN UNREASONABLE HOUR, OK?
HEY, DAD, I JUST KNOCKED OFF A BANK AND MY FACE IS PLASTERED ALL OVER THE 11:00PM NEWS
...AND THE FRONT COVER OF TODAY'S EDITION OF THE DEVIL'S ADVOCATE.
HEY, DAD, I WANT TO BECOME A PRIEST AND DO MISSIONARY WORK IN THE ISLANDS.
YOU'RE ALL GROUNDED.
GOOD ONE DAD, CATCH YA LATER.
THAT'S PUTTING YOUR ROOT DOWN, FRED!
YA... WHAT DO YOU KNOW?
I KNOW THAT I WANT A DIVORCE, MR. PREMATURE POLLINATION!

EVERYONE PLEASE
RISE FOR THE HONORABLE
JUDGE FATE...
FATES COURT ROOM....
MRS. POSSESSED FLOWER.
PLEASE TAKE THE STAND.
MRS. POSSESSED FLOWER.
CAN YOU TELL THE COURT WHY
YOU WOULD LIKE A DIVORCE?

OBJECTION, YOUR HONOR...
COUNCIL IS LEADING THE WITNESS.
OVER RULED.
FRED WAS NICE AT FIRST. BUT SOON INTO THE MARRIAGE, HE BECAME INSENSITIVE. HE NEGOTIATED HALF OF MY FAMILY OUT OF THEIR SOULS WITH HIS STUPID CONTRACTS. MY UNCLE LESTER IS NOW THE BEST-USED CAR SALESMAN ON THE PLANET...
JUST IMAGINE HOW LITTLE SOUL HE WILL RETAIN WITH A DEAL LIKE THAT.

THAT'S A LOAD
OF POT SOIL!...
AT THE
VERY LEAST,
IRRELEVANT.
SPECULATION
YOUR HONOR.
ONE MORE OUT BURST,
MR. POSSESSED FLOWER AND
I'LL FIND YOU IN CONTEMPT!
YOU ARE SO WISE AND FAIR,
JUDGE FATE. MY MOTHER ALWAYS
TOLD ME THAT I SHOULD
HAVE DATED A JUDGE.

THIS IS FLAGRANT FLIRTATION! SHE IS TRYING TO INFLUENCE THE COURT!
ALL OF THIS HOSTILITY IS MAKING ME TENSE.
I THINK I HAVE HEARD ENOUGH. THE VERDICT IS AS FOLLOWS...
MRS. POSSESSED FLOWER WILL TAKE FULL CUSTODY OF ALL OF HER CHILDREN... AND IN ORDER TO TAKE PROPER CARE OF HERSELF AND HER SOLARIUM FULL OF KIDS...
SHE WILL BE ENTITLED TO HALF OF FRED THE POSSESSED FLOWER'S INCOME.
THIS COURT IS ADJOURNED!
CRACK!!!

JUDGE FATE, FOR THE LOVE OF YOU KNOW WHO, I'M BEGGING YOU TO RECONSIDER!
YOUR HONOR!, IF YOU TICKLE MY CLIENT, DOES HE NOT LAUGH?
IF YOU PRICK MY CLIENT, DOES HE NOT OOZE THAT STICKY, PLANT STUFF?
ALL DECISIONS ARE FINAL. PERHAPS YOU WOULD LIKE TO DISCUSS THIS MATTER WITH CUPID.
I DO BELIEVE THAT HE IS USUALLY AT THE ROOT OF THESE THINGS.
SERIOUSLY!

SOMEWHERE ON EARTH...
TRUST ME...
I WOULD MAKE AN EXCELLENT CASTING DIRECTOR.
ZAP!!!
CUPID!!!

IT WASN'T MY FAULT. LOUIE TOLD ME TO DO IT.
POW!!!
WHY WOULD LOUIE PUT YOU UP TO THIS?
HE JUST THOUGHT THAT YOU NEEDED SOME COMPANY. HE WAS ONLY TRYING TO BE A FRIEND.
YEAH, I GOTTA MILLION FRIENDS LIKE LOUIE. IT WOULD BE MUCH EASIER IF I ONLY HAD A COUPLE.

LOUIE'S DEN
HI FRED, CHECK OUT MY NEW...
SLAM!

SHUT UP! I GOT A BONE TO PICK WITH YOU. WHY THE HELL DID YOU GIVE CUPID INSTRUCTIONS TO SHOOT ME WITH ONE OF HIS ARROWS?

I HAVE NO COMMENTS ON THAT SITUATION... AT THIS TIME.

IF YOU WEREN'T MY BOSS, I'D TURN YOUR SORRY BUTT OVER TO THE *HUMANITY CORPORATION* AND LET THOSE SICK BASTARDS HAVE THEIR WAY WITH YOU!

BACK AT FRED'S OFFICE....

MY KIDS ARE HOPELESS DEGENERATES. MY WIFE SPLIT WITH HALF OF MY STUFF AND I'M NOT ON SPEAKING TERMS WITH MY BEST FRIEND.

BLAM!!!

IT WAS ALL JUST A NIGHTMARE.
I AM ALONE...
6:66
NO WIFE?
NO KIDS?...
NO FRIENDS?..
WHAT A PERFECT WORLD!
THE END

HAPPY PREDATOR PUBLICATIONS
HAPPY NICK'S
FRED the POSSESSED FLOWER
6
"THE ORIGIN OF FRED"
GUEST STARRING:
GOD & SATAN

THE ORIGIN OF FRED
WELCOME TO HELL, LADIES AND GENTLEMEN. TODAY YOU WILL WITNESS THE ORIGIN OF FRED THE POSSESSED FLOWER, AS TOLD BY ME... LOUIE. THE STORY BEGINS FOREVER AGO, IN A PLACE THAT I'M SURE THAT YOU ARE ALL FAMILIAR WITH...

... HEAVEN.
CREATED, WRITTEN and ILLUSTRATED by: HAPPY
SO WHAT DO YOU GUYS WANT TO DO TODAY?
LET'S SEE IF YOU CAN BREAK YOUR RECORD AND MAKE A PLANET IN LESS THEN EIGHT DAYS.
YOU'RE ON.
FRED The POSSESSED FLOWER

CALL ME VAIN, BIG GUY, BUT I THINK THAT I DESERVE TO BE YOUR EQUAL.
I DON'T THINK SO, LOUIE.
WHAT DO YOU MEAN?... YOU DON'T THINK SO! I AM THE MOST BEAUTIFUL AND INTELLIGENT ANGEL THAT YOU HAVE EVER CREATED! I WANT TO BE THE BEST!
MICHAEL, KICK THIS BUM OUT.
OK, LOUIE...
YOU'RE OUTTA HERE.
MIKE, YOU CAN'T DO THIS TO ME!

COME ON GUYS,
CAN'T WE DISCUSS
THIS?
AUSTA LA
VISTA, LOUIE.
WELL THIS IS JUST FINE!
I'LL OPEN UP MY OWN PLACE!
I THINK THAT I WILL GO WITH
A FIREY, SKULLY, BOILING
TAR MOTIF.

DECORATING AND RENOVATING WAS A CHALLENGE.
ALL OF MY FRIENDS HELPED ME MOVE IN.

CLEANING EVERYTHING UP WAS A LOT OF HARD WORK.
FIXING THE PLACE UP WAS EXHAUSTING. SO I DECIDED TO GO AND GRAB A BITE TO EAT.
GARDEN of EDEN FRUIT MARKET
BAKERS DOZEN OF APPLES $6.66
I HAD HEARD THAT THIS PLACE HAD THE BEST FRUIT, ANYWHERE.

WHEN I HAD GOT THERE, THERE WAS ONLY ONE APPLE LEFT AND A NAKED WOMAN TOO. SHE LOOKED HUNGRY SO I ACTED LIKE A GENTLEMAN...
LADIES FIRST.
I ADMIRED THE LANDSCAPE OF THE GARDEN AND DECIDED THAT I WOULD PLANT A GARDEN OF MY OWN, IN HELL.
I'LL HAVE THE ANGEL HAIR PASTA, WITH A SIDE ORDER OF DEVILED HAM...

I PLUCKED A SINGLE LEAF FROM ONE OF EDEN'S MANY FLOWERS...
... THEN I PLANTED IT IN MY BACKYARD.
WITHIN NO TIME, THE FLOWER GREW...
... SO I NAMED HIM, FRED. HE WAS THE CUTEST, LITTLE, POSSESSED FLOWER, THAT YOU COULD EVER SEE.
I KNEW FROM THE START THAT FRED HAD WHAT IT TOOK TO SOME DAY FOLLOW IN MY FOOTSTEPS.
F IS FOR FEAR
R IS FOR RAGE
E IS FOR EVIL
D IS FOR THE DEWEY DECIMAL SYSTEM

JUST B.C....
I STARTED TO CONSULT WITH FRED ON A DAILY BASIS.
WHAT SHOULD I DO WITH MY SHARES IN THE ROMAN EMPIRE? I NEED A GOOD STOCK TIP.
SELL... IT'S GOING TO FALL. THEY'LL ALL BE LOOKING TO THE BIG GUY FOR SALVATION. WE SHOULD GET OUT NOW.
FRED PROVED TO HAVE IMPECCABLE RELIABILITY AND A SHREWD MARKETING SENSE.
FRED WAS SHARP AND HAD AN EXCELLENT MIND FOR ADVERTISING.
LOUIE, WHAT DO YOU THINK ABOUT HAVING SOME SPOKESMEN FOR HELL?
A GROUP OF EVIL SANTA'S ELVES, SO TO SPEAK. SOMETHING IS MISSING? CAN ANY OF YOU RIDE HORSES?
OK?
DEATH
PESTILENCE
TIME
FAMINE

ADVERTISING WAS A VERY SMART MOVE, ON FRED'S BEHALF. WITH THE FEAR OF HELL SO HEAVILY PROMOTED...
... WHEN PEOPLE DIED, THEY WOULD BE WILLING TO SELL THEIR SOULS, TO NOT BE INCINERATED.
HELL STARTED TO MAKE A HUGE PROFIT ON HOLY REDEMPTION RATES. WE WERE, AND STILL ARE MAKING A KILLING. NO PUN INTENDED.

FOR A WHILE, FRED WAS IN CHARGE OF RECRUITING AND TRAINING NEW HELL EMPLOYEES.
OK, CLASS... WHO CAN NAME THE SEVEN SINS?
WHAT?... WHERE?... WHEN?...
I DIDN'T HAVE TIME TO STUDY... I HAVE A NOTE FROM MY MOTHER.
HI THERE, MR. FLOWEEEEER.
OH, OH! PICK ME!
AS FRED'S CAREER PROGRESSED, HE ACTED AS LIAISON BETWEEN ALL OF THE ALIEN, SUBSIDIARY, HELLS BELONGING TO THE MILLIONS OF PLANETS THROUGHOUT THE UNIVERSE AND BEYOND.
HOW'S EVERYBODY'S DARK SIDE OF THE FORCE, THIS EVENING?
HOLINESS IS HIGHLY ILLOGICAL.
PHONE HELL.

WHILE FRED WAS ON THE OTHER SIDE OF THE GALAXY...
HEAVEN IMPLEMENTED ITS STRONGEST PROMOTION, TO DATE, TELEVANGELISTS. HELL'S RATINGS STARTED TO PLUMMET AT A DANGEROUS RATE. MORE PEOPLE THEN EVER WHERE GOING TO HEAVEN. THE BIG GUY WAS IN HIS GLORY, AS HE WATCHED HELL START TO CRUMBLE.
YOUR PAIN HAS A NAME AND IT IS GRUMPY, OLD FART SYNDROME!
AMEN!
LOVE-SWEEEEET!
I RECKON THAT WE WASTE NOT... HEY YOU, IN THE FRONT ROW... ARE YOU GONNA FINISH THAT CHOCOLATE BAR?
I... REVEREND LOVE-SWEET, HAS GOTS A REQUEST... DON'T WORRY, BE HOLY!

HELL'S BOARDROOM...
THIS SUCKS!
SOON AFTER THE LAUNCH OF THE TELEVANGELISTS, HEAVEN IMPLEMENTED VARIOUS, FOLLOW-UP SHOWS LIKE...
... DRIVEWAY TO HEAVEN...
...THE TEN DEMANDMENTS...
YOU MUST OBEY!
OR DIE!
... AND THE DAVID AND GOLIATH SHOW...
I'M DISGUSTINGLY CUTE... AREN'T I, GOLIATH?
YOU'RE RIGHT, DAVIE.

WHAT ARE WE GOING TO DO?
WE HAVE ALREADY RELEASED OUR OWN SHOWS AND MOVIES...
BUT THEY ARE ALL USELESS!
LET'S GO PLUNDER EUROPE, PILGRIM...
I MEAN PAGAN.
GANGUS KAHN
STARRING: JOHNNY WAYNE

HELL'S VERSION OF THE TEN DEMANDMENTS DIDN'T HAVE ANY EFFECT ON SOCIETY, EITHER!
I LIKED THEM.
1. THOU SHALL LET CREDIT CARD COMPANIES GET AWAY WITH RIDICULOUS INTEREST RATES.
2. THOU SHALL HAVE THE RIGHT OF WAY ON THE ROAD, IF THY IS DRIVING A TRANSPORT TRUCK.
3. THOU SHALL CREATE AN UNREALISTIC IMAGE OF THE IDEAL WOMAN.
4. THOU SHALL BORROW THY NEIGHBOR'S LAWN MOWER AND NEVER RETURN IT.
5. THOU SHALL SKATE ON THIN ICE WHILE PLAYING WITH FIRE.
6. THOU SHALL DISREGARD SOLAR POWER AND UNNECESSARILY BURN FOSSIL FUEL.
7. THOU SHALL COVET THY NEIGHBOR'S WIFE.
8. THOU SHALL LOVE BULK HOGAN, EVEN IF HE DID TURN INTO A BAD GUY.
9. THOU SHALL RESPECT ALL POLITICIANS.
10. THOU SHALL CONSIDER SCHMOOZING MORE IMPORTANT THEN ACTUAL TALENT.

WE COULD PUT A FOOLISH AND GREEDY VALUE ON MONEY, SO THAT WHEN SOCIETY WRECKS THE EARTH, BEYOND ALL RECOGNITION...
... SOCIETY WILL NOT BE ABLE TO AFFORD THE TECHNOLOGY THEY WILL NEED IN ORDER TO COLONIZE MARS.
NO.. THAT IS TOO LONG TERM. I NEED A PLAN THAT IS STRONG ENOUGH TO DISCREDIT HEAVEN AND THE BIG GUY. IMMEDIATELY!
I'M BAAAAACK!
CLICK!
SO, AM I TO UNDERSTAND THAT HELL IS IN DIRE NEED OF INCREASING POPULARITY AND GAINING MARKET SHARE?

AND, AM I TO UNDERSTAND THAT NOT ONE OF HELL'S ACCOUNT EXECUTIVES CAN COME UP WITH A PROMOTIONAL CAMPAIGN TO GIVE HEAVEN SOME REAL COMPETITION?...
... EH, TOOTH FAIRY?
WELL DON'T WORRY, LOUIE, I HAVE A PLAN.
LET ME GET THIS STRAIT... TELEVANGELISTS ARE AT THE ROOT OF OUR PROBLEMS. WELL, WHAT BETTER WAY TO FIGHT TELEVANGELISTS, THEN WITH A NEW TELEVANGELIST.
I THINK THAT YOU ARE CRAZY.
ZAP!
SERIOUSLY?
SOMEWHERE FAR AWAY...
ALL POLKA RADIO
SOMETIMES, FRED CAN BE SO MEAN...

BACK IN HELL'S BOARDROOM...
AS I WAS SAYING...
WE WILL SPOIL HEAVEN'S CROP. WE WILL TAINT THE PUBLICS PERCEPTION OF TELEVANGELISTS IN GENERAL.
MEMBERS OF THE BOARD...
INTRODUCING HELL'S TELEVANGELIST, TIMMY TAGGERT!
I AM TIMMY TAGGERT, MY BROTHERS AND SISTERS. THE BIG GUY HAS SPOKEN TO ME IN A VISION. HE WANTS ME TO TELL THE PEOPLE WHAT THEY NEED...
JESUS SALT AND PEPPER SHAKERS, FOR ONLY THREE HOLY PAYMENTS OF $6.66...
... ORDER NOW AND RECEIVE A SET OF BURNING HEDGE SHOWER CURTAINS, FREE!!!

IF YOU BUY TWO PAIRS OF LEVITE JEANS, FOR $30.00 EACH AND GET A THIRD PAIR FOR ONLY $29.99!!!
IF YOUR SINS HAVE BEEN UNFORGIVABLE AND YOU WANT TO SECURE A PLACE IN HEAVEN... YOU CAN NOW ORDER HEAVENLY INSURANCE.
SECURE YOUR PLACE BESIDE THE BIG GUY WITH A REGULAR MONTHLY PAYMENT OF $6.66... OR PERHAPS, JOIN THE BIG GUY'S FAN CLUB FOR THE SAME MONTHLY RATE.
SOMEWHERE IN SUBURBIA... AT SOME WANNA BE SUPERHERO'S APARTMENT...
LOCO BANANAS!
WHO THE HELL DOES THIS, TIMMY TAGGERT THINK HE IS?
IT'S WOW!!!!MAN AND HORNY THE FISH... A SUPERHERO CREATION OF HAPPY AND COLLEGUES THAT NEVER TOOK OFF... PITTY...
EXACTLY... WHO THE HELL, INDEED?

DAYS LATER,
IN A NIGHT CLUB...
... SOMEWHERE.
... WHEREVER.
YOU DANCE WELL, FOR A TELEVANGELIST.
THANKS BABY...
YOU THREE LADIES MAKE ME WANT TO SIN MY BRAINS OUT!
WAITRESS, ANOTHER ROUND OF HOLY WALL-BANGERS FOR THE LADIES AND I.

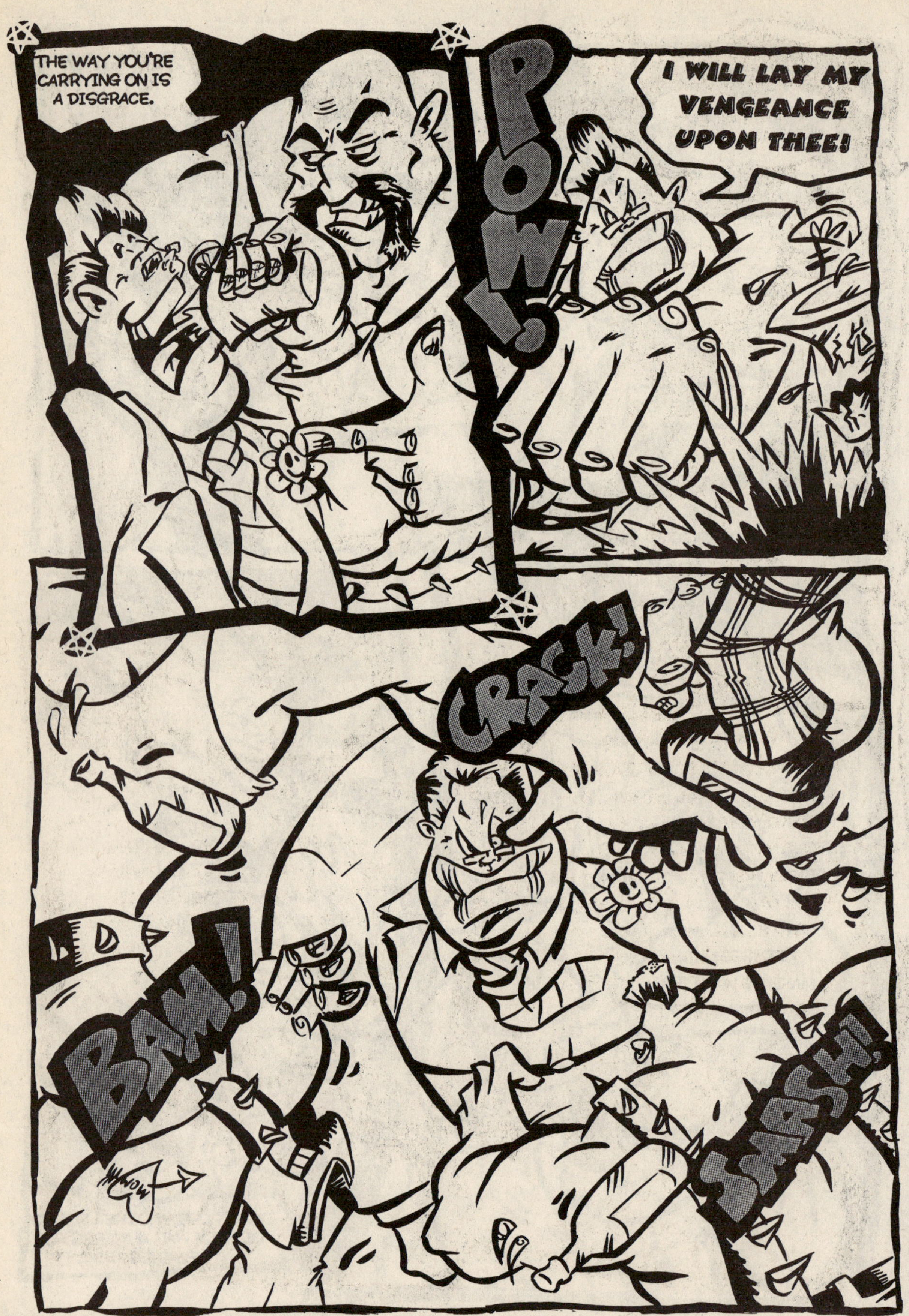

THE WAY YOU'RE CARRYING ON IS A DISGRACE.
POW!
I WILL LAY MY VENGEANCE UPON THEE!
CRACK!
BAM!
SMASH!

TIMMY TAGGERT, YOU HAVE THE RI...
YOU HAVE THE RIGHT TO GO HELL!
I LOVE THIS GUY.
THE WORLD RENOWNED, TELEVANGELIST, TIMMY TAGGERT HAS BEEN CHARGED WITH PUBLIC DRUNKENNESS, ASSAULT CAUSING BODILY HARM, ASSAULT WITH A DEADLY WEAPON, ASSAULTING A POLICE OFFICER, PUBLIC MISCHIEF AND HE HAS BEEN CAUGHT FRATERNIZING WITH PROSTITUTES.
HE HAS ALSO BEEN CHARGED WITH MARKETING FRAUD AND IS CURRENTLY UNDERGOING A GOVERNMENT AUDIT. THIS MEANS NO MORE HOLY MERCHANDISE FOR ANYBODY. TIMMY TAGGERT IS A BAD SEED READY TO BE PLANTED IN JAIL FOR A VERY LONG TIME.

HELL'S BOARDROOM...
TIMMY TAGGERTHAS SAVED HELL FROM IMMINENT BANKRUPTCY!...
AND IT WAS ALL ATTRIBUTED TO FRED THE POSSESSED FLOWER!
HELL'S STOCK VALUE IS INCREASING BY THE SECOND. ACCORDING TO OUR LATEST SURVEYS, OUR RATINGS ARE RAPIDLY CLIMBING!
#1 !!!
JUST THINK HOW HELL'S MARKET SHARE WILL SKYROCKET WHEN TIMMY TAGGERT ANNOUNCES TO THE WORLD THAT THE BIG GUY HAS FORGIVEN HIM FOR HIS SINS...
AND THEN HE REPEATS HIS ACTIONS SEVERAL TIMES OVER.
YOU ARE BRILLIANT!

...PRESENT DAY...
...LOUIE'S GREEN HOUSE
NOW FRED HANDLES ALL OF HELL'S BUSINESS AFFAIRS ON MY BEHALF. AS THE SPOKESMAN OF HELL AND SEMI-RETIRED OWNER, I SPEND MOST OF MY TIME RELAXING, AND TENDING TO MY FULL TIME HOBBY, GARDENING.
SO THERE YOU HAVE IT, LADIES AND GENTLEMEN... THE ORIGIN OF FRED THE POSSESSED FLOWER.
THE END

WHAT IF HELL FROZE OVER AND FRED THE POSSESSED FLOWER COMICS WERE FORBIDDEN?
SERIOUSLY?!

HAPPY PREDATOR PUBLICATIONS
HAPPY NICK'S
FRED the POSSESSED FLOWER
7
"GOD IS FROM VENUS, THE DEVIL IS FROM MARS"
YOU'RE LOOKING HEAVENLY THIS EVENING.
KISS!!!
KISS!!!
KISS!!!
GUEST STARRING: GOD & SATAN

"GOD IS FROM VENUS, THE DEVIL IS FROM MARS"
Creator Writer Illustrator HAPPY NICK
FRED the POSSESSED FLOWER
HELL'S OBSERVATORY....
I AM GOING TO SHARE A SCANDALOUS STORY ABOUT THE FUNNIEST PLACE IN EXISTENCE...
DIMENSION #1... OTHERWISE, COSMICALLY REFFERED TO AS THE PLAY GROUND OF THE HIGHER PURPOSE. THIS IS WHERE THE FORCES OF GOOD AND EVIL CONSTANTLY BATTLE FOR SUPERIORITY IN A MOST ENTERTAINING FASHION.
YOUR EARTH NOT ONLY EXISTS IN DIMENSION #1... IT IS ALSO THE FEATURE ATTRACTION.

COME ON, LINCOLN III!
WHATZ ZA MATTA VIS YOU?! YOU ARE ZA KING!!!
ETERNITY STARTS AND STOPS FOR ALL OF US AT DIFFERENT TIMES. IT IS THE DURATION OF A SOUL'S EXISTANCE.
THE LIVING CONSIDER ETERNITY TO BE FOREVER. HOWEVER, THE LIVING DON'T KNOW MUCH AT ALL.
AS FAR AS THE COSMOS ARE CONCERNED, ETERNITY IS A GAME TO BE PLAYED.
WHY, YOU ASK? WELL... WHAT YOU'RE REALLY ASKING IS THE MEANING OF LIFE...

THE ANSWER IS ACTUALLY QUITE SIMPLE... FINISH THE GAME!
HOW YOU ASK?...
LET ME JUST TELL YA!
IF YOUR SOUL CAN SUCCESSFULLY BE RE-INCARNATED INTO EVERY FORM OF LIFE ON EVERY PLANET IN EVERY UNIVERSE OF EVERY DIMENSION... IT WILL ATTAIN A FULLFILLED EXISTANCE AND BE ELIGIBLE FOR IT'S HIGHER PURPOSE.
AND YOU THOUGHT THAT A BAR EXAM WAS HARD.
THE REALLY BIG QUESTION IS, WHY FINISH THE GAME?
IT'S TO ACCOMPLISH THE HIGHER PURPOSE. WHAT IS THE HIGHER PURPOSE, YOU ASK, OH INQUISITIVE, EARTHLING INFESTATION?
IT IS TO EITHER INHERIT OR CONQUER ONE OF THE TWO COSMIC VOCATIONS.
THAT OF GRAND DEVIL OR ALMIGHTY GOD!
I WAS JUST NOTICING THAT IF THERE WAS ANYMORE PANELS ON THIS PAGE, IT WOULD BE MICROPHEESH.

HEAVEN...
GOD!!! OH MY GO...SH! IT'S REALLY YOU! CAN I GET YOU A COLD BEVERAGE OR PERHAPS A LIGHTENING BOLT?
NO THANKS, BURNING HEDGE,
WHAT BRINGS YOU HERE MY DARLING WIFE? I CAN'T REMEMBER THE LAST TIME THAT YOU CAME TO THE OFFICE.
BIG GUY, I AM CONCERNED WITH ONE OF OUR PLANETS ORBITING IN DIMENSION #1... EARTH... SINCE EARTH AND ALL OF ITS INHABITANTS ARE ONLY AT THE FIRST STAGE OF RE-INCARNATION AND HAVE NEXT TO NO SPIRITUAL OR LIFE EXPERIENCE...
DO YOU THINK THAT IT'S WISE TO GIVE THEM SO MUCH TECHNOLOGY SO FAST?
WHAT ARE YOU TALKING ABOUT?
I'M REFFERING TO ALL OF THE DAMAGE THAT THEY HAVE DONE WITH WARS, POLLUTION AND PRIME TIME TV...
WHAT'S NEXT?
RELAX, HONEY... THEY MIGHT BE A TAD AGGRESSIVE, BUT EQUALLY AS PASSIONATE.
I HOPE SO FOR YOUR SAKE. YOU'RE THEIR BABYSITTER!
YES DEAR.

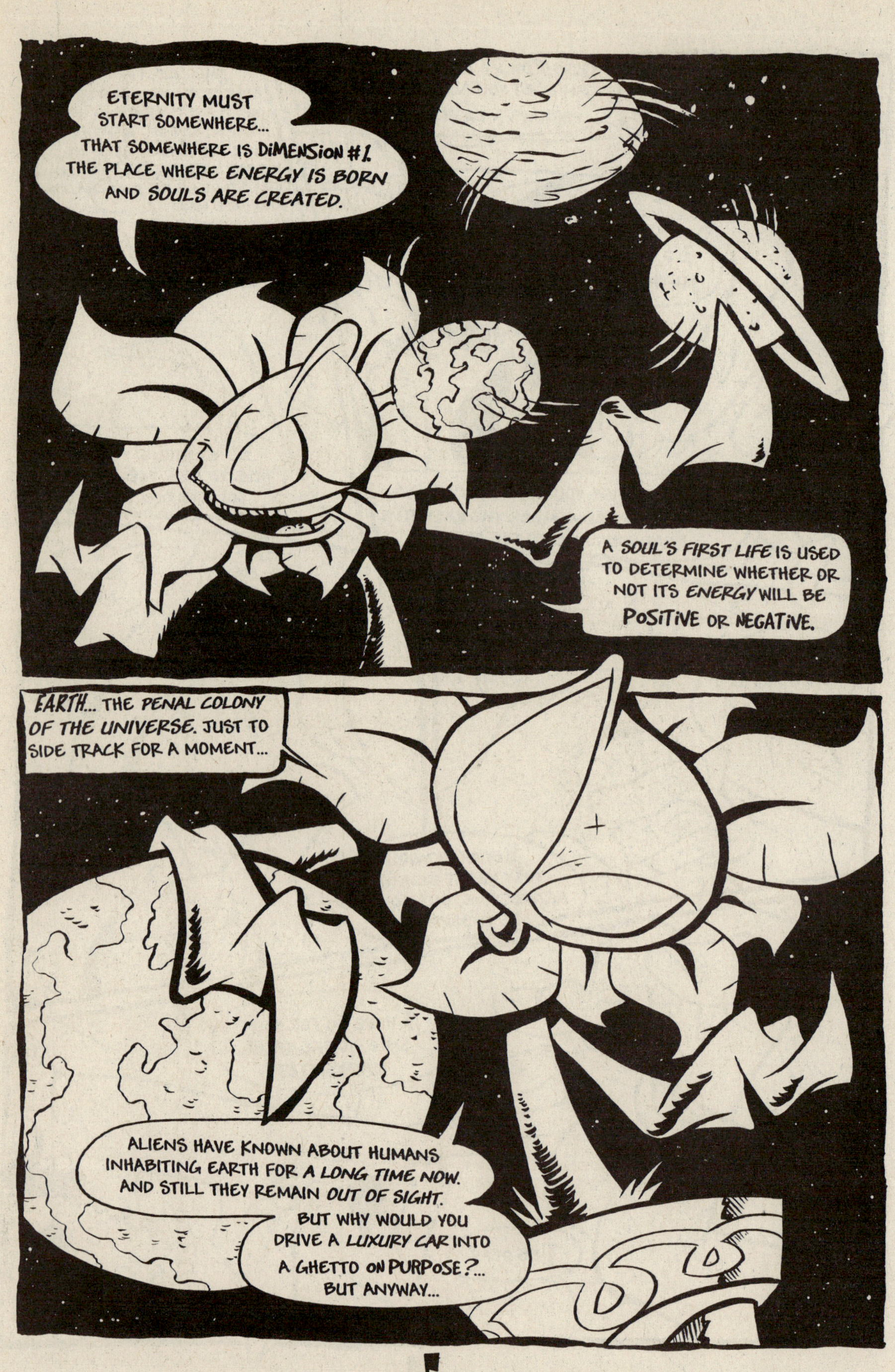
ETERNITY MUST START SOMEWHERE... THAT SOMEWHERE IS DIMENSION #1. THE PLACE WHERE ENERGY IS BORN AND SOULS ARE CREATED.
A SOUL'S FIRST LIFE IS USED TO DETERMINE WHETHER OR NOT ITS ENERGY WILL BE POSITIVE OR NEGATIVE.
EARTH... THE PENAL COLONY OF THE UNIVERSE. JUST TO SIDE TRACK FOR A MOMENT...
ALIENS HAVE KNOWN ABOUT HUMANS INHABITING EARTH FOR A LONG TIME NOW. AND STILL THEY REMAIN OUT OF SIGHT.
BUT WHY WOULD YOU DRIVE A LUXURY CAR INTO A GHETTO ON PURPOSE?... BUT ANYWAY...

IT WAS COL. MUSTARD IN THE STUDY WITH THE CANDLE STICK!
WAS NOT!
WAS TOO!
WAS NOT!
SOUNDS LIKE BOLSHEVIK TO ME!
THAT'S IT, NOW YOUR TOAST!
CLICK!
THE JEHOS MIGHT BE RIGHT!
ZING!
D-DAY!!...

BY THE END OF YOUR SOUL'S FIRST LIFE IS WHEN ITS ENERGY IS BRANDED AS POSITIVE OR NEGATIVE... GOOD OR EVIL. IT IS THEN, WHEN YOUR SOUL WILL EITHER GO TO HEAVEN OR HELL.
OBVIOUSLY, I PREFER THE LATTER SO DOES MY BOSS, LUCIFER.
DOOMSDAY!... THE MOST WONDERFUL TIME OF THE YEAR!

HEY, BOOGIMAN... WHAT PERCENT OF THE SOULS OF HUMANITY DID WE ACCUMULATE IN THE DOOMSDAY PROMOTION?
90.666%!!!
THIS IS GREAT! NOW I DON'T HAVE TO PAY FOR TEETH ANYMORE! NOW I CAN JUST YANK ALL THE FREE TEETH I WANT OUTTA EVERYONES BURNT CARCASAS!
CAN YA FEEL THE LOVE?!

HEAVEN?..
THE BIG GUY MIGHT RUN EARTH... BUT SHE!...GOD!.. IS IN CONTROL OF EVERYTHING!
UNFORTUNATELY FOR THE BIG GUY, IT'S THAT TIME OF THE MONTH WHEN GOD'S MOON SHINES THE FULLEST.
HOLD STILL, FRANK!
DON'T TELL THIS CAT WHAT TO DOOD!

MEN!?!
WHAT DO YOU MEAN THAT YOU ACCIDENTALLY DESTROYED EARTH?!
I CAN'T BELIEVE THAT YOU THREW THAT BLACK HOLE AT ME! MY PARENTS GAVE US THAT FOR A WEDDING GIFT!
I TOLD YOU NOT TO GIVE HUMANS SO MUCH KNOWLEDGE ALL AT ONCE!
GAAK!!!
WHAT DO YOU HAVE TO SAY FOR YOUR SELF, FOR HEAVEN'S SAKE?!
OOPS...

THAT'S IT!... I'M SICK OF YOU NEVER LISTENING! I AM INDEFINATELY SUSPENDING YOUR DUTIES AS REGIONAL GOD OF DIMENSION #1
BUT, BU...
GET OUT!!!
I AM INCHARGE OF THE FIRST HEAVENLY DIMENSION AND THIS IS HOW I AM TREATED?... NO RESPECT!
SLAM!!!
GOD?... HONEY?...

AS YOUR SOUL PROGRESSES, RE-INCARNATION INTO ADVANCED DIMENSIONS WILL ALLOW OPPORTUNITIES TO ARRISE.
INSTEAD OF BEING A CUSTOMER IN HEAVEN OR HELL, YOU MIGHT BECOME AN EMPLOYEE.
WITH EMPLOYMENT COMES A CHAIN OF COMMAND. THERE ARE VARIOUS LEVELS OF HOLY AND SATANIC AUTHORITY THROUGHOUT THE DIMENSIONS.
FOR EXAMPLE, SUPREME BEINGS, REGIONAL GODS AND DEVILS, LIKE THE BIG GUY AND LOUIE... NOT TO MENTION ANGELS, DEMONS AND EVEN POSSESSED FLOWERS!

SOMEWHERE DEEP INSIDE THE FINAL DIMENSION OF HELL...
EVIL EVENING, LADIES AND DEVILS... I THE GRAND DEVIL, HAVE SUMMONED ALL OF YOU, THE REGIONAL DEVILS FROM EVERY DIMENSION OF HELL TO...
WHERE'S LUCIFER?
YA, WHAT ABOUT LUCIFER?
EXCLUDING LUCIFER.
WHY IS LUCIFER EXCLUDED?
I'M GETTING TO THAT!
WHAT THE HELL ARE YOU SUPPOSED TO BE ANYWAY?... AN ANT EATER?
A FLYING REINDEER?
¡I'M A MOSQUITO!!! I'M THE GRAND DEVIL... WHAT ELSE IS MORE EVIL THEN A MOSQUITO?! THINK ABOUT IT.
BILLZI BART!!!

I HAVE PREPARED A SPEECH... TWO RABBIS AND A ROCK STAR WALK INTO A BAR... WHAT?!
I'M GONNA RE-KILL MY SPEECHWRITERS.
AS I WAS SAYING...
I WANT TO DISCUSS THE FATE OF HELL, AS IT PERTAINS TO DIMENSION NUMBER ONE.
666
YOU MEAN THE MOST EVIL AND FUN PLACE IN ALL OF EXISTENCE!
THAT'S THE PLACE.

WE HAVE ALL WORKED HARD, KEEPING EACH OF OUR ASSIGNED DIMENSIONS IN TIP TOP SHAPE...
WHY SHOULD WE LET LUCIFER, AN X-ANGEL OF ALL PEOPLE RUN THE MOST LUCRATIVE DIMENSION OF HELL?!
WHY SHOULD WE LET LUCIFER HAVE ALL OF THE FUN?!
LUCIFER ISN'T JUST GONNA HAND OVER HIS HELL TO US...
AND WHAT ABOUT HIS RIGHT HAND PLANT, FRED THE POSSESSED FLOWER? HE'S A MEAN LITTLE SUCKER!
SCREWTAPE, DON'T BE SUCH A BABY
I HAVE ALREADY THOUGHT OF THAT AND I HAVE FOUND A DELICIOUSLY, iRONIC SOLUTiON.
BARNY
THE POSSESSED FLOWER!!!

THERE IS MUCH MORE TO THE *DAILY RUNNING* OF THE *COSMOS*, WHICH I HAVE NEGLECTED TO MENTION IN MY NUT SHELL EXPLANATIONS.
FOR EXAMPLE... **PEOPLE WHO NEED PEOPLE!**

MIKE! GABE! YOU GUYS GOTTA HELP ME. JUST TALK TO HER!
I'D RATHER CAST DOWN LUCIFER AGAIN!..
NO WAY! SHE MAKES ARTHUR SEEM FRIENDLY.
FLICK!
SOME HELP.
MT. SIANI...
PLEASE?!
THOU SHALL NOT INTERFER WITH THE BIG GUY'S CHICK.
I'D LOVE TO HELP YA' BOSS, BUT GOD HITS BELOW THE BELT AND I'D LIKE TO HAVE SAPPLINGS SOME DAY.
BAD DEITY!!!
SOLID GOLD, VERY HEAVY!
WHY HAS THOU FORESAKEN ME?!
WELL, FINE!

JUST REMEMBER THE COSMIC CLICHE, BOYS AND GIRLS... ALL'S FAIR IN LOVE AND WAR...
LUCIFER'S HOUSE, SOMEWHERE IN HELL...
ALRIGHT!... "AS THE SPACESHIP TURNS!"
FORGET ABOUT HER NUMBER ONE, SHE'S ENGAGED!
DING DONG!
GRAND DEVIL, WHAT A SURPRISE... FROD, IS THAT YOU?
NAH-AH!
HEY, BIG "D"... I LIKE THAT HUMMING BIRD LOOK ON YOU.
HE'S A MOSQUITO FOR CHRIST'S SAKE!

LUCIFER, I'D LIKE YOU TO MEET MY SIDEKICK.
BARNY THE POSSESSED FLOWER!
WHAT THE HELL IS GOING ON HERE?!
YOUR HELL IS WHAT'S GOING ON HERE.
OR SHOULD I SAY, MY HELL!
WHAT ARE YOU TALKING ABOUT?!
DON'T YOU GET IT, YOU DORK? YOU'RE FIRED!
BUT REST ASSURED, LUCIFER..
I DO HAVE AN ALTERNATIVE HELL FOR YOU.

BASIC HIGH SCHOOL FRENCH CLASS...
CE'S QUE SAY WHAT?
HELP!!! JE MA PELLE LUCIFER.
COUCH POM DE TERRE!
FRED'S PRIVATE SOLARIUM... JUST A FEW INTERDIMENSIONAL MILES AWAY FROM PURGATORY...
SILLY, LITTLE CARTOONS...
FRED
DING DONG!

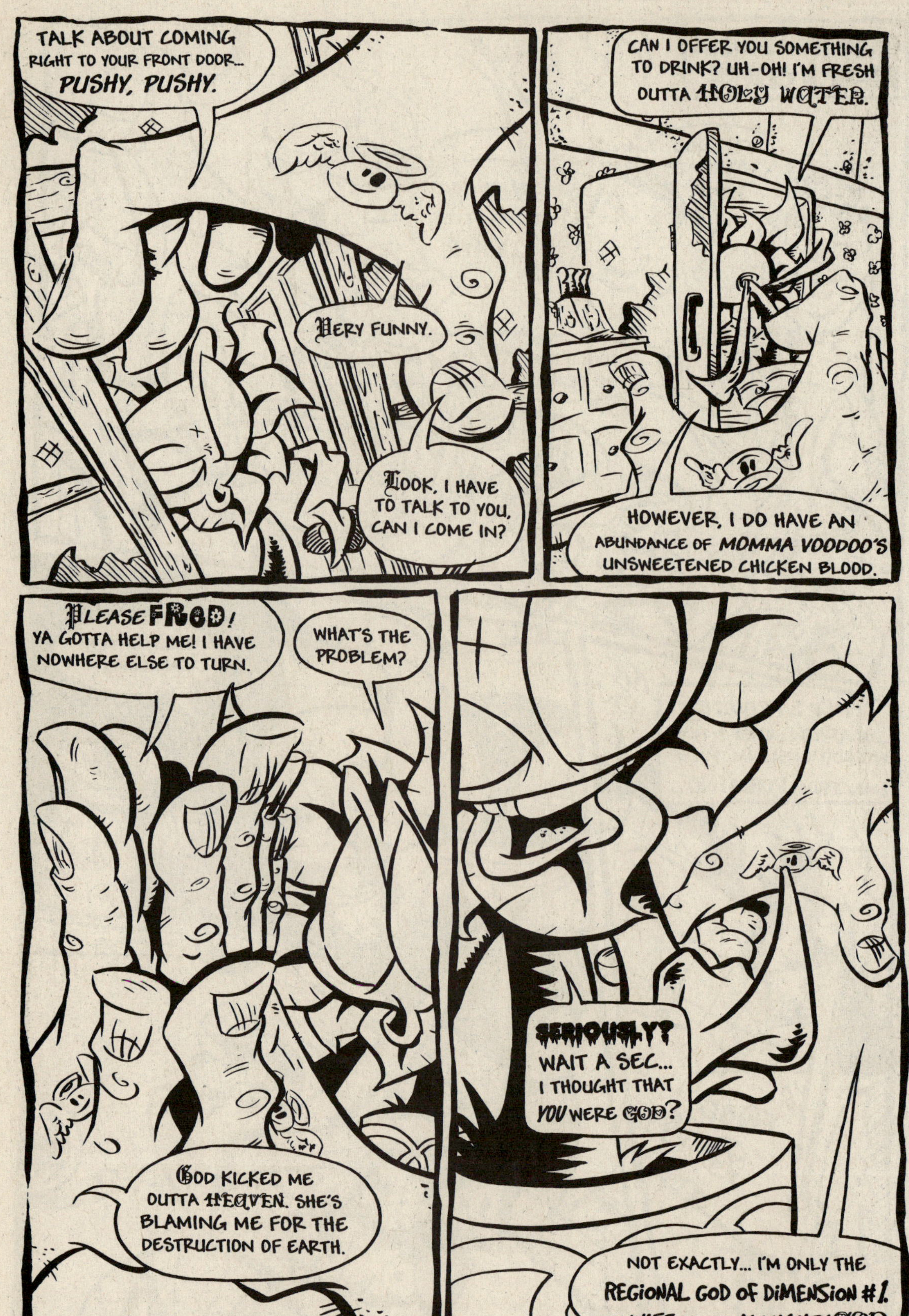

TALK ABOUT COMING RIGHT TO YOUR FRONT DOOR... PUSHY, PUSHY.
VERY FUNNY.
LOOK, I HAVE TO TALK TO YOU. CAN I COME IN?
CAN I OFFER YOU SOMETHING TO DRINK? UH-OH! I'M FRESH OUTTA HOLY WATER.
HOWEVER, I DO HAVE AN ABUNDANCE OF MOMMA VOODOO'S UNSWEETENED CHICKEN BLOOD.
PLEASE FROD! YA GOTTA HELP ME! I HAVE NOWHERE ELSE TO TURN.
WHAT'S THE PROBLEM?
GOD KICKED ME OUTTA HEAVEN. SHE'S BLAMING ME FOR THE DESTRUCTION OF EARTH.
SERIOUSLY? WAIT A SEC... I THOUGHT THAT YOU WERE GOD?
NOT EXACTLY... I'M ONLY THE REGIONAL GOD OF DIMENSION #1. MY WIFE IS THE ALMIGHTY GOD.

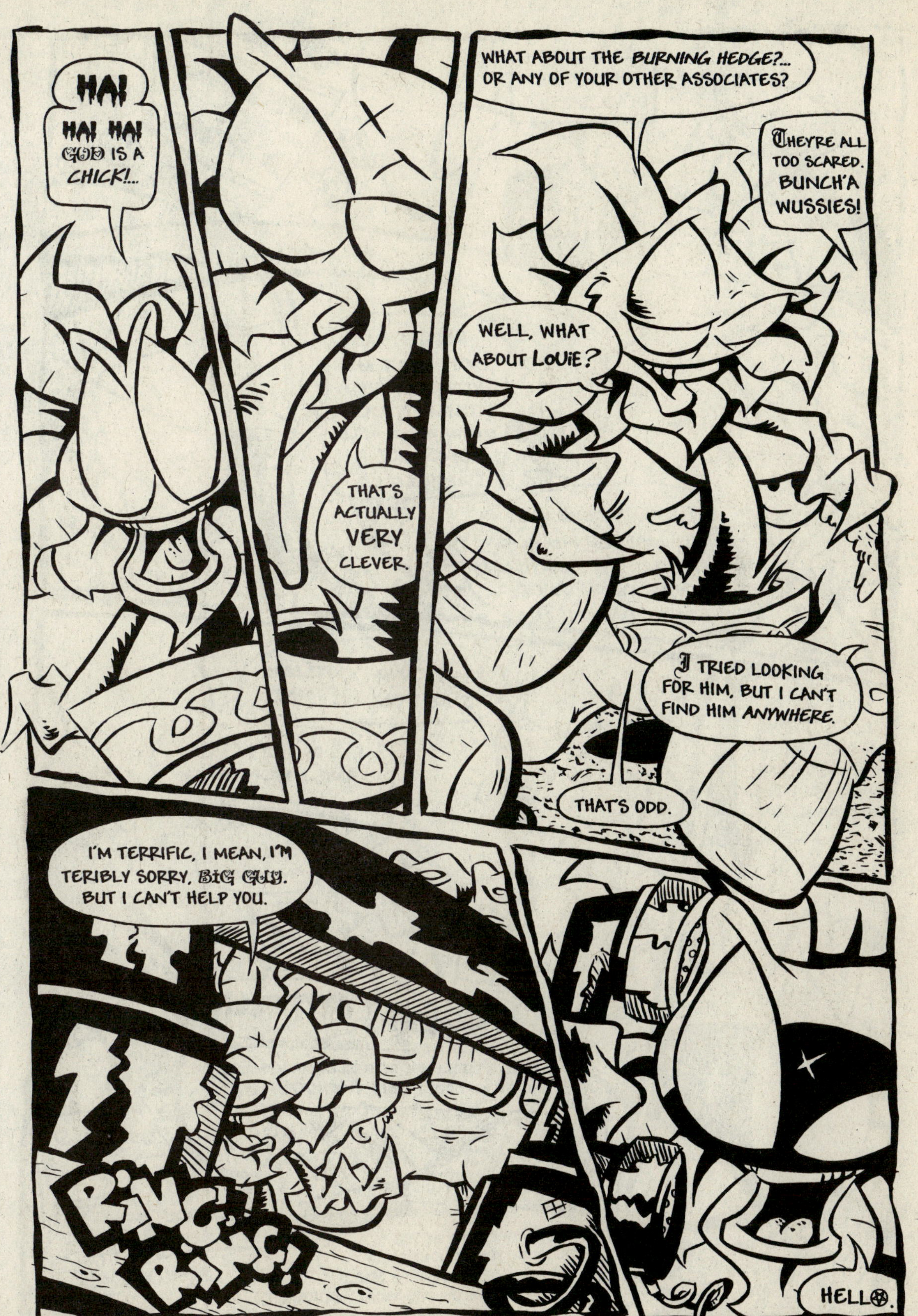
HA!
HA! HA!
GOD IS A CHICK!...
THAT'S ACTUALLY VERY CLEVER.
WHAT ABOUT THE BURNING HEDGE?... OR ANY OF YOUR OTHER ASSOCIATES?
THEY'RE ALL TOO SCARED. BUNCH'A WUSSIES!
WELL, WHAT ABOUT LOUIE?
I TRIED LOOKING FOR HIM, BUT I CAN'T FIND HIM ANYWHERE.
THAT'S ODD.
I'M TERRIFIC, I MEAN, I'M TERIBLY SORRY, BIG GUY. BUT I CAN'T HELP YOU.
RING! RING!
HELLO.

THE GRAND DEVIL'S JAIL...
WHEE-HELL OF FORTUNE
FRED, YA GOTTA GET ME OUTTA HERE! I'M STUCK IN A PLACE THAT MAKES OUR HELL LOOK LIKE A COUNTRY CLUB.
THE GRAND DEVIL HAS DEVIL-NAPPED ME! HE IS TRYING TO TAKE OVER OUR HELL! DO SOMETHING QUICK, DEVIL DAMN IT!!!
DON'T WORRY LOUIE, I HAVE AN IDEA. BUT IN THE MEANTIME, DON'T DROP THE PERVERBIAL SOAP.
THIS BRAND-"X" PIZZA IS... DARE I SAY, DIVINE.
YA.... OK, BIG GUY... I HAVE A PROPOSITION.
I'LL DO ANYTHING!
ANYTHING?!
I HAVE A LITTLE BIT OF A DILEMMA MYSELF... MAYBE WE COULD HELP EACHOTHER OUT.
GOD IS PISSED AT YOU BECAUSE YOU ACCIDENTALLY LET MOST OF HUMANITY'S SOULS SLIP INTO HELL ON DOOMSDAY... CORRECT?

HERE'S MY PROBLEM... THE GRAND DEVIL HAS IMPRISONED LOUIE AND IS IN THE MIDST OF AMALGAMATING MY HELL INTO HIS OWN DIMENSION. HERE'S WHAT I PROPOSE...
IF I WAS TO REFUND ALL OF THE DOOMSDAY SOULS... WHICH WOULD RESTORE HUMANITY AND PUT YOU BACK INTO THE GRACE OF GOD...
IN RETURN, YOU WILL HELP ME FIRE THE GRAND DEVIL AND REPLACE HIM WITH LOUIE. I WANT THE GRAND DEVIL TO BURN IN HEAVEN!
WHY DON'T YOU WANT HELL FOR YOUR SELF? YOU COULD DO A MUCH BETTER JOB THEN THAT IDIOT, LOUIE.
HMMM?
I COULDN'T DO THAT TO LOUIE... HE'S MY BEST FRIEND.
BESIDES, I RUN THINGS DOWN HERE HOW I SEE FIT ANYWAY. IF I EVER SCREW UP, HOWEVER UNLIKELY THAT IS...
HE WOULD MAKE AN EXCELLENT SCAPEGOAT.
HA! HA! HA! HA! HA!
HA! HA! HA!

THE GRAND DEVIL'S JAIL... DURING VISITING HOURS...
I HAVE WORKED OUT A DEAL WITH THE BIG GUY TO STRAITEN THIS WHOLE MESS OUT.
YOU'RE THE BEST FLOWER A DEVIL COULD HAVE!
IT HAS TAKEN A LOT OF MY PATIENCE TO PUT UP WITH THE BIG GUY FOR THE LAST COUPLE OF DAYS. SINCE HE DIDN'T HAVE A PLACE TO STAY, I LET HIM CRASH ON MY COUCH.
HE'S SO ANNOYING, ALWAYS WHINING ABOUT HIS ESTRANGED WIFE, GOD. I'M TEMPTED TO JUST KICK HIM OUT AND VOID OUR AGREEMENT!
SAY WHAT?!

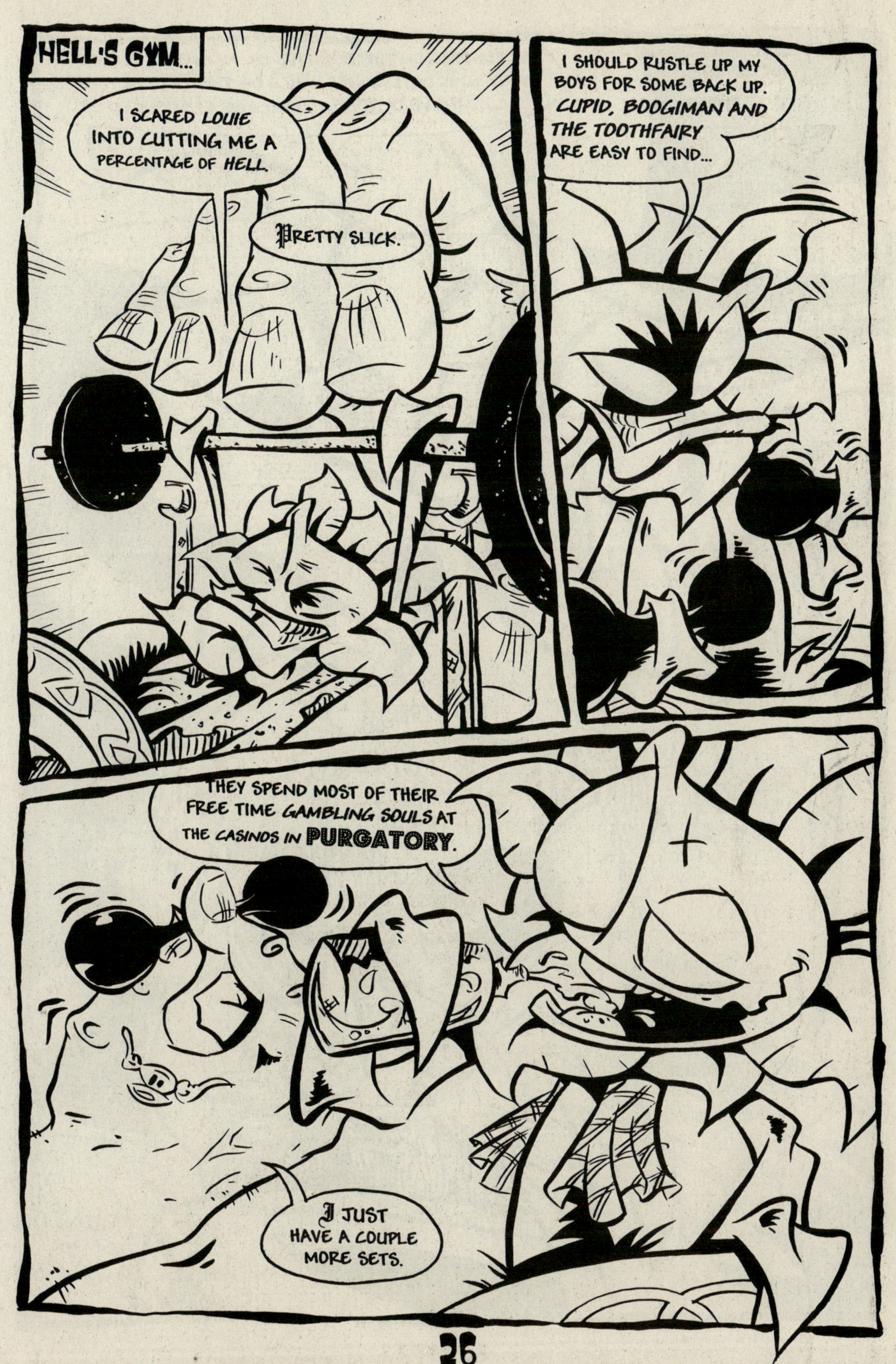
HELL'S GYM...
I SCARED LOUIE INTO CUTTING ME A PERCENTAGE OF HELL.
PRETTY SLICK.
I SHOULD RUSTLE UP MY BOYS FOR SOME BACK UP. CUPID, BOOGIMAN AND THE TOOTHFAIRY ARE EASY TO FIND...
THEY SPEND MOST OF THEIR FREE TIME GAMBLING SOULS AT THE CASINOS IN PURGATORY.
I JUST HAVE A COUPLE MORE SETS.

DEPENDING ON THE POSITIVE OR NEGATIVE NATURE OF YOUR SOUL DETERMINES WHICH OF THE TWO, ULTIMATE, COSMIC VOCATIONS YOU WILL BE BEST SUITED FOR.
FATHER...
FATHER...
OHHH BE QUIET FOR CHRIST'S SAKE!
OOPS.. WAS THAT BLASPHEMY, A FREUDIAN SLIP OR JUST PUN?

SATAN'S PALACE
HEAVENLY MIRAGE
STYX RIVIERA
IF THE POSITVE AND NEGATIVE ENERGY IN YOUR SOUL IS TOO EVENLY BALANCED YOU MUST BE SENT TO PURGATORY...
PURGATORY IS A PLACE WHERE FATE ORGANIZES DESTINY AND DECIDES WHETHER OR NOT IF YOU WILL BECOME A GOOD GUY OR A BAD GUY.
IT'S YOUR LUCKY DAY, MOTHER-T AND LADY-D.
DEALER LOSES, YOU CAN CASH YOUR CHIPS IN FOR HEAVENLY ADMITTANCE COUPONS AT THE CHANCE BOOTH.
...WHICH LIES JUST BEYOND THE REALM OF LIFE, SOMEWHERE BETWEEN THE BOARDERS OF DIMENSION #1 AND #2.
HOW'D YOU BOYS LIKE TO EARN SOME TIME AND A HALF?

To eternity and beyond!
ON SLASHER, ON CANCER, ON DISHONOR, ON BLITZKREIG. ON VOMIT, ON STUPID, ON MANSON, ON NIXON!!!
I AIN'T SCARED OF THE GRAND DEVIL.
YO YO SUCKA, WORD! SUBTITLE: I AM INCLINED TO DISAGREE.
AMEN! HE SCARES THE BABY FORMULA OUTTA ME!

THE LAST DIMENSION OF HELL...
HOW IN THE HELL ARE WE GONNA GET INSIDE?
OPEN
LEAVE THAT TO ME!!!
IT'S RAINING DEMONS! ALLELUIA!!!
EVIL JOB, CUPID.

I'LL FIND LOUIE, BIG GUY, YOU TAKE THE BOYS AND WARM UP THE GRAND DEVIL FOR ME.
OKI DOKI, FROD.
CRASH!
WHAT IN THE LAST DIMENSION OF HELL?!

KA-POW!
$
I'VE ALWAYS WONDERED WHAT TOOTH CHANGE WAS GOOD FOR.
NOW YA KNOW.
OUCH!
I MEAN IT...

MEANWHILE...
I TOT I TAW A POSSESSED FLOWER!
YOU DID! YOU DID!
ARGL!
GARK!
SAY MERCY YOU WIMP!
GIVE IT UP YOU BLASPHEMING WOODPECKER!!!
OWW!
I'M A MOSQUITO, DAMN IT!!!
YOU THINK THAT PURPLE DINOSAURS ARE ANNOYING, BUT I'LL BE THE DEATH OF YA!

TA DAAA!!!
THAT'S THE SECOND, DAMN DOOR THAT THEY'VE WRECKED!
I WAS SAVING THESE FOR THE BURNING HEDGE, BUT YOU'RE AN EVEN BIGGER WEED!
SNIP!
AHH!

GO AHEAD, MAKE MY DAY, PAGAN.
?
BANG!
OHHH TAY!
I THINK THAT YOU WERE ROD KING, IN A PAST LIFE, YOU STUPID SEA HORSE.
THAT'S CLOSE, BUT FOR THE LAST TIME... I'M A FREAKIN' MOSQUITO!!!
OUCH! OWWW! OOOH!
BOOZE
XXX

WE WARMED HIM UP FOR YA.
NOW FINISH HIM OFF!
DOWN THE HATCH.
NOOO!!!
GULP! BURP! ... SPICY?
THE GRAND DEVIL IS GONNA GIVE ME MORE GAS THEN IF I ATE AT TACOHELL!

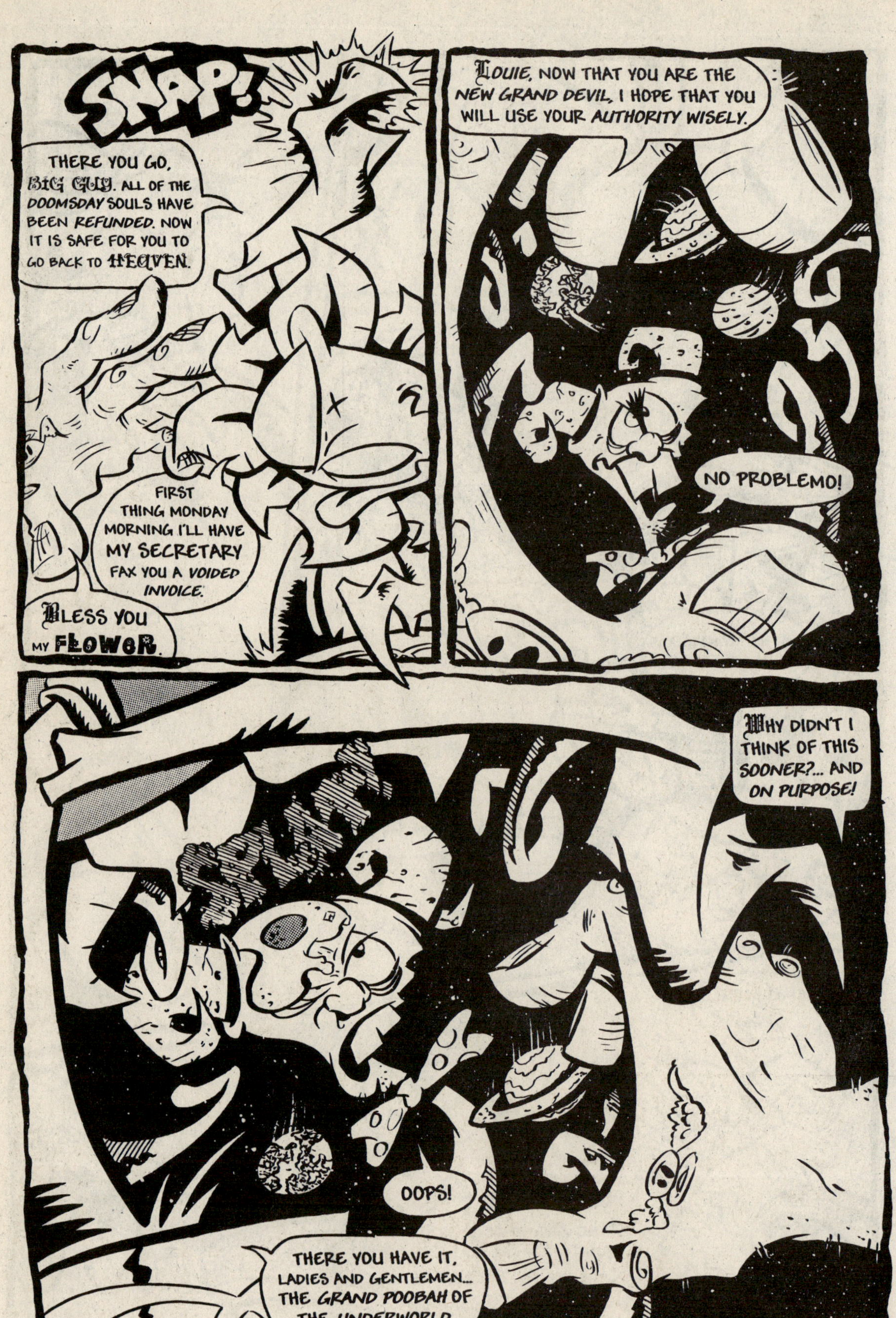
SNAP!
THERE YOU GO, BIG GUY. ALL OF THE DOOMSDAY SOULS HAVE BEEN REFUNDED. NOW IT IS SAFE FOR YOU TO GO BACK TO HEAVEN.
FIRST THING MONDAY MORNING I'LL HAVE MY SECRETARY FAX YOU A VOIDED INVOICE.
BLESS YOU MY FLOWER.
LOUIE, NOW THAT YOU ARE THE NEW GRAND DEVIL, I HOPE THAT YOU WILL USE YOUR AUTHORITY WISELY.
NO PROBLEMO!
WHY DIDN'T I THINK OF THIS SOONER?... AND ON PURPOSE!
SPLAT!
OOPS!
THERE YOU HAVE IT, LADIES AND GENTLEMEN... THE GRAND POOBAH OF THE UNDERWORLD.

IT IS AMUSING AND IRONIC HOW THE FORCES OF GOOD AND EVIL COLABORATE TO GET WHAT THEY WANT.
IT'S FUNNY, YET SICKENING HOW THEY NEED EACHOTHER.
KA-CHH!
i HATE YOU GUYS... A LOT!!!

HONEY BEAR!
CUTIE PIE!
BUT THAT IS NOT THE END...
YOUR SOUL THEN EMBARKS ON A JOURNEY OF RE-INCARNATING INTO A ZILLION NEW LIFEFORMS WITHIN A ZILLION NEW DIMENSIONS.
EMOTIONALLY ENTER AT YOUR OWN RISK!
VISITING HIGHER DIMENSIONS OF HEAVEN AND HELL INBETWEEN EACH LIFE...
UTILIZING PAST EXPERIENCES AS COSMIC, CORRESPONDENCE LESSONS ON YOUR QUEST FOR THE HIGHER PURPOSE.
...OR PERHAPS WHEN YOU DIE... THAT'S THE END?!

HAPPY PREDATOR PUBLICATIONS
HAPPY NICK'S
FRED the POSSESSED FLOWER
8
"LL COOL JESUS"
HOW DOES IT LOOK SO FAR?
GUEST STARRING: GOD & SATAN

"LL COOL JESUS"
YOU CAN'T ARGUE THAT TWO PLUS TWO EQUALS FOUR, OR THAT MR. "BURT AND THE BANDIT" REYNOLDS, WEARS A RUG. IT IS ALL UNQUESTIONABLE FACT. BUT ART!... NOW THAT IS BASED UPON TASTE. IT IS SUBJECTIVE, NOT TO MENTION PRETENTIOUS AND CHAOTIC... I LIKE THAT.
FRED the POSSESSED FLOWER
HELL'S GALLERY... THE LUEV-CIFER...
EXIT to eden
admition $6.66
Creator Writer Illustrator HAPPY NICK

HELL'S BOARDROOM...
WE NEED A NEW PROMOTION THAT WILL BRING A LARGE RESPONSE TO HELL'S IN-STORE TRAFFIC. SOMETHING WITH A WIDE DEMOGRAPHIC GROUP, SO THAT WE CAN SATURATE THE MARKET. WE NEED TO GET OUR HANDS ON SOME FRESH SOULS, PEOPLE! MY CONTACTS AT HUMANITY INC. INFORM ME THAT PREDJUDICE AND RACISM ARE VERY EFFECTIVE METHODS OF GENERATING FOWL AND IGNORANT EMOTIONS. THAT'S JUST WHAT WE NEED TO PICK UP SALES.
SO LET'S TRY TO UTILISE THESE CONCEPTS AS THE THEME FOR OUR NEXT PRODUCT LAUNCH.
FAITH
HOW ABOUT IRREVOCABLE PROOF THAT JESUS WAS BLACK?

THAT SHOULD SEND THE WHITE TRASH OF THE TWENTIETH CENTURY INTO A FRENZY... AND PREVOKE BLACK PEOPLE TO REBEL!
WE COULD SEGREGATE AND CONQUER! WITH BOTH SIDES ON THE OFFENSIVE... EACH TASTING THE SIN SOAKED DELICACIES OF RAGE, JEALOUSY, SHAME, ETC. ALL OF WHICH ARE SPECIAL ENTRÉES IN HELL'S MENU.
WHITE PEOPLE HAVE BEEN THE RACIAL BULLIES SINCE MODERN MAN'S EXISTENCE. THEY'RE NOT GOING TO ACKNOWLEGDE THIS WHETHER IT IS TRUE OR NOT.
AND BLACK PEOPLE ARE AN ANGRY RACE, THEY'RE JUST LOOKING FOR A GOOD REASON TO ATTACK!
AND RIGHTFULLY SO.
WHY IS THAT?
HAVEN'T YOU EVER SEEN ROOTS... OR BLAZING SADDLES?
HOW COULD WE PULL OFF A SCAM OF THAT MAGNITUDE?
LIKE THIS...

PRESENT DAY... SOMEWHERE WHERE THE PROMISEDLAND IS SUPPOSED TO BE...
HEY, CHRIS! COME HERE, QUICKLY! I'VE FOUND SOMETHING!
WHAT IS IT, HAILY?
SOME SORT'A SECRET TOMB!
THIS IS ST. PETE'S LONG, LOST, SECRET SHRINE OF JESUS MEMORABILIA!
ST. PETE'S LONG, LOST, SECRET SHRINE OF JESUS MEMORABILIA.
THE ONLY THING THAT JESUS EVER GAVE ME WAS THIS STUPID T-SHIRT
JESUS ROCKS
JESUS #1
WHAT TIPPED YOU OFF?

WHO THE HELL IS THAT?
I THINK THAT WHAT HE MEANS IS, WHO THE HEAVEN IS THAT?
THIS PAINTING HAS AN INSCRIPTION.
IT READS... A PORTRAIT IN YOUR HONOR. TO JESUS, MY NUMBER ONE FAN. YOUR LOYAL APOSTLE AND FAVORITE DRINKING BUDDY, PETE.
THERE'S MORE...
IS IT AUTHENTIC?
P.S. YES, THIS PICTURE IS AUTHENTIC.
TO MAKE SURE, WE SHOULD CARBON DATE IT.
P.S. AGAIN, CARBON DATE IT IF YOU MUST.

HA! HA! HA!
HA!
HA!
WE SHOULD GO STRAIT TO THE PRESS WITH THIS! THE WORLD MUST KNOW THE TRUTH!!!
WAIT, WE CAN'T RUSH INTO ANYTHING! WE'VE GOT TO STOP AND THINK. AS MUCH AS I'D LIKE TO TELL THE TRUTH... IN THIS CASE, THE TRUTH MIGHT DO MORE HARM THEN GOOD. WE COULD EXPERIENCE GLOBAL CHAOS AND PANDEMONIUM!
WE'LL BE FAMOUS!!!
YOU'RE RIGHT! TABLOIDS, HERE WE COME!!!

THE VATICAN...
YA THINK I COULD EVER RECEIVE THE iMPERMATER?
OPEN
INSIDE THE BIG V...
THESE PORNO RUBEX CUBES ARE SURE FRUSTRATING!
A BLINDING, HEAVENLY LIGHT.
WHAT THE HE...
AH, AH, AH... WATCH YOUR MOUTH, BLASPHEMER.
FATHER W
I CAN'T BELIEVE MY OWN TWO EYES. AM I DREAMING?!
YOU DUMMY! YOU DEDICATE YOUR ENTIRE LIFE TO WORSHIPPING ME WITH ZERO PROOF OF MY EXISTENCE...
AND NOW THAT YOU FINALLY GET TO SEE ME FIRST HAND... NOW YOU'RE SKEPTICAL? PUTZ.

I DID NOT MEAN TO OFFEND YOU, FATHER.
HEY, DON'T WORRY ABOUT IT... AND CALL ME, BIG GUY.
NOW LISTEN UP, WE HAVE A VERY SERIOUS SITUATION HERE. TWO ARCHEOLOGISTS HAVE DISCOVERED THE LONG LOST PORTRAIT OF JESUS, PAINTED BY ST. PETE.
THAT'S WONDERFUL!!! WHAT A FASCINATING DISCOVERY!
AN ACTUAL, ACCURATE PORTRAIT OF JESUS... SPECTACULAR!
THIS IS NOT GOOD NEWS AT ALL YOU MORON!
BUT BIG GUY, NOW THE PEOPLE CAN FINALLY SEE THE TRUE FACE OF THE SON OF GOD!!!

THE PAINTING IS OF A BLACK MAN.
HOLY SHI-TZU!!!
YOU SAID IT!
NOW I NEED YOU TO RETRIEVE THAT PAINTING BEFORE THE WORLD GETS THE SHOCK OF A LIFE TIME.
AS PITIFUL AS IT SOUNDS, HUMANITY IS NOT MATURE ENOUGH TO DEAL WITH SUCH A TRUTH. IT WILL SEND THEM INTO CHAOS.
LOUIE IS GONNA HAVE A FIELD DAY WITH THIS.
WHO?
THE DEVIL, YOU IDIOT! HOW THE HEAVEN DID YOU EVER GET THIS JOB WITH THAT PEA BRAIN OF YOURS? DID YOU HAVE TO SLEEP YOUR WAY TO THE TOP, OR SOMETHING?
NO COMMENT.

I AM STILL CONFUSED AS TO HOW THAT DAMN PAINTING IS ACTUALLY REAL. I'M THE ONE AND ONLY BIG GUY, I'M SUPPOSED TO KNOW EVERYTHING FOR ST. PETE'S SAKE!
I KNOW THAT IT WAS QUITE AWHILE AGO, BUT I'M PRETTY SURE THAT MY KID WAS JUST A HONKY WITH A NICE TAN.
WHAT IF THE CHURCH SIMPLY DENIES THE AUTHENTICITY, LET ALONE THE EXISTENCE OF THE PAINTING?
YOU'VE GOT SOMETHING ON YOUR SHIRT.
WHERE?
FLICK!!
GOTCHA... SEE HOW GULLIBLE HUMANS ARE? THEY'LL BELIEVE ANYTHING THAT THE TABLOIDS HAVE TO SAY.

FRED... HOW DID YOU MAKE THAT FORGED PAINTING OF JESUS SO CONVINCING?
EASY... IT'S REAL.
WHATCHA TALKIN' ABOUT, FROD!
I WENT BACK IN TIME TO 21 A.D. JUST DAYS AFTER JESUS TURNED OF LEGAL AGE...
JERUSALEM 90210
I DIDN'T DO TOO MUCH REALLY. I JUST PLANTED SOME FOOD FOR THOUGHT...
GREAT IDEA, TURNING ALL OF THIS WATER FROM THE VARIETY STORE INTO WINE, JESUS.
BURP!... THANKS, PETE.

HEY JESUS, I'VE GOT A HILARIOUS IDEA... PEOPLE WILL BE BAFFLED FOR YEARS TO COME. BURP!
OH YA, WHAT'S THAT?
FOR A JOKE, WHY DON'T YOU PAINT JESUS AS A BLACK GUY?
BACK IN HELL...
VERY CLEVER, FRED.
I'M GONNA SEND THE BOYS TO RUN INTERFERENCE, JUST IN CASE THE BIG GUY GETS INVOLVED.

BACK AT THE BIG-V-...
JUST INCASE YOUR PEOPLE CAN'T OBTAIN THE PAINTING IN QUESTION, I'M GOING TO LEAVE YOU MY BEST MAN TO SUPERVISE YOUR MISSION.
SNAP!
THE FATHER, THE SON AND NOW... THE HOLY CO-HOST!!!
HELLO ... YOUR IMMANENCE HOW IS MY FIRST CONTESTANT?
OH MY GOD! YOU'RE THE HOLY CO-HOST!
PLEASE ANSWER IN THE FORM OF A QUESTION.

OK YOUR IMMANENCE, FOR THE EXTRA BONUS ROUND... UNBOISTLY, HISTORICALLY AND GEOGRAPHICALLY, WE HAVE ASCERTAINED THAT JESUS COULD NOT HAVE BEEN BLACK.
DISREGARDING ST. PETE'S PAINTING, OF COURSE.
CAN YOU TELL ME JESUS' TRUE HERITAGE? AND REMEMBER... ANSWER IN THE FORM OF A QUESTION.
WHAT IS... MIDDLE EASTERN.
AAAAAA!!! WRONG! JESUS WAS AN ALIEN, JUST LIKE ELVIS AND WEBSTER.
JESUS' BROTHER WAS SUPPOSED TO COME IN THE YEAR 2000 AND AVENGE HIM.
HE HAD AN OPENING IN HIS SCHEDULE, SO HE CAME A FEW YEARS EARLIER.
ARE YOU TELLING ME THAT THE MESSIAH IS ALREADY HERE, ON EARTH?!
HE WAS, BUT HIS SPACESHIP MALFUNCTIONED AND CRASHED IN ROSWELL DURING THE 40'S.

ROSWELL, HANGER 666...
POP!
SNEAKY, ALIEN BASTARD!!!
AND AGAIN, THE BIG "V"...
WHAT IN THE HEAVENS WAS MY POINT TO THAT LITTLE TANGENT?... OH WELL, I CAN'T REMEMBER.
BEATS ME.

IN A PLACE... WHERE EVER ARCHEOLOGISTS HANG OUT...
I HAVE THE LONG, LOST, AUTHENTIC PAINTING OF JESUS!... AND HE'S BLACK!!!
THERE'S NO SMUT OR VIOLENCE, BUT IT STILL SOUNDS JUICY.
I'M JUST AS BAD AS HERALDO, MAYBE EVEN WORSE.
THIS SOUNDS COOL, BUT YOU SUCK, BITE ME! SHOCK VALUE!
I WONDER IF JESUS' MR HAPPY WAS BIGGER THEN MINE?
HEY, I'M OPRAH... NEED I SAY MORE?
THIS SOUNDS SO EXCITING! I NEED A HUG.
HERE ARE THE TOP TEN NOT FUNNY REASONS WHY YOU SHOULD BE A GUEST ON MY SHOW...

SO WHAT WAS THE RESPONSE LIKE?
OUTSATNDING!!! ALL OF THE TALK SHOWS AND NEWS WANT US!
BUT GET THIS... THE TABLOIDS TURNED US DOWN.
WHY?!
...BECAUSE THEY ONLY EXCEPT FICTION... GO FIGURE? THEY DID HOWEVER, ASK ME IF I HAVE EVER BEEN ABDUCTED OR IF I HAVE ANY ENVIRONMENTALLY INDUCED, PHYSICAL MUTATIONS.
HELL'S SPA...
DAMN TABLOIDS!!! THEY NEVER CO-OPERATE WHEN YOU NEED THEM TO.
I LIKE TINY BUBBLES!

THE NOSEY BASTARD
TABLOID MAGAZINE

THE NOSEY BASTARDS,
EDITOR-IN CHIEF'S OFFICE...

YOU WILL IGNORE THE PROSPECTS OF THE TWO ARCHEOLOGISTS *OR ELSE!!!*

THE TALKSHOW PERSONALITIES MIGHT BE *TOO POWERFUL* FOR ME TO PUSH AROUND... BUT YOU ARE STILL WITHIN MY REACH.

SCUM

I CAN'T WIN! LAST WEEK *THE DEVIL* WAS IN HERE THREATENING ME, AND NOW YOU!

ULTIMATUMS FROM THE BOOGIMAN, REPREMANDS FROM THE BURNING HEDGE AND JUST AWHILE AGO, I WAS YELLED AT BY AN EVIL, LITTLE FLOWER.
THIS ISN'T FUN AT ALL... AND I USED TO THINK THAT STOCK BROKERS AND AIR TRAFFIC CONTROLLERS HAD HIGH STRESS JOBS.
AND HE WAS A MEAN SUCKER TOO!
DON'T BE SUCH A BABY.
SOMEWHERE IN THE CITY...
CHRIS, DID YOU HEAR SOMETHING?
NOPE.

WE'RE BEING ATTACKED BY NINJAS!!!
STAY TUNED!!! SAME POSSESSED COMIC!!! NEXT POSSESSED PAGE!!!

UH, EXCUSE ME... WE ARE HOLY NINJAS!
HOW BIBLICALLY INCORRECT.
OH YA, WELL WHO ASKED YOU, GRASSHOPPER?!
HOW'S THAT?
WE BENEFIT THIS STORY!
ADDING NINJAS TO A STORY IS LIKE SPRINKLING PARMESAN CHEESE ON FETTUCINI ALFREDO... WE ADD AN EXTRA, LITTLE SOMETHING.
WHATEVER.
STOP CHANGING THE SUBJECT AND HAND OVER THE PAINTING...
OR WE'LL BE FORCED TO BREAK OUT THE OVER EXAGGERATED COMBAT SOUND EFFECTS!
AND THEN KICK YOUR BUTTS!

HEAVEN'S HOLY SQUASH COURT...
LOUIE, DID YOU REALLY THINK THAT YOU WOULD GET AWAY WITH THIS PAINTING NONSENSE?
I DON'T KNOW WHAT YOU ARE TALKING ABOUT.
I KNOW THAT IT COMES NATURALLY TO YOU, BUT DON'T PLAY STUPID WITH ME.
THIS WHOLE CONSPIRACY HAS YOUR SIDEKICK, FROD The POSSESSED FLOWER, WRITTEN ALL OVER IT.
WHERE IS THAT LITTLE CROSS POLINATED DEMON, ANYWAY?
UUMMMM?...

BACK IN THE CITY...
I'VE GOTTA INTERFER ON PRINCIPAL ALONE. I MEAN SERIOUSLY? GIVE ME A BREAK... HOLY NINJAS?... WHAT HAPPY IDIOT THINKS OF THESE THINGS?
ZAP!!!
I'LL DEAL WITH KARI-KARI, LARRY AND MOE WHILE YOU TWO GET THAT PAINTING TO THE MEDIA
?

THANKS, WHOEVER YOU ARE.
MY PLEASURE, SWEETHEART. NOW SCRAM.
BE CAREFUL, LITTLE FLOWER!
YOU TWO KIDS GO AND HAVE FUN, DON'T WORRY ABOUT A THING.
THIS GUARDIAN ANGEL STUFF IS A FUN PLACE TO VISIT, BUT I WOULDN'T WANT TO LIVE HERE.
GAAK!!!
OWWW!!!
YELP!!!
SOON AFTER..
THAT WAS TASTY... BUT I'LL BE HUNGRY AGAIN IN A HALF AN HOUR.

ZOINK!!!
THE HOLY CO-HOST?
TWO CAN PLAY AT THIS GAME, FRED. IF YOU CAN INTERFER, THEN SO CAN I. WHAT DO YOU THINK ABOUT THAT?!
WELL... SINCE YOU'RE THE V.P. of BRAND "Y", AND I'M THE V.P. of BRAND "X"... I SAY THAT WE JUST KICK THE HEAVEN AND HELL OUTTA EACHOTHER.
WORKS FOR ME.
AH HA! FRED The POSSESSED FLOWER!!! I KNEW THAT YOU WERE BEHIND ALL OF THIS!
TAKE THAT, YOU GAMESHOW DEITY!!!
YA! WE KNEW THAT YOU WERE BEHIND ALL OF THIS!
BURNING HEDGE, PLEASE...
I SHOULD WARN YOU THAT I'M THE GUY WHO CREATED THE GUY WHO INVENTED WEED WACKERS!!!

BIG GUY, I CAN EXPLAIN. IT'S REALLY QUITE AMUSING. I'M SURE THAT YOU'LL GET A KICK OUT OF IT IF YOU JUS...
ENOUGH!!! TIME FOR YOU TO PAY!
YA, ... TIME FOR YOU TO PAY!
ONE OF THESE DAYS I'M GONNA TRIM THAT ANNOYING, LEAFY ASS OF YOURS INTO A BONZAI tree!
GULP ...
FOR 666 POINTS, CAN YOU TELL ME WHAT HEAVENLY WRATH ARE WE GOING TO INCURR ONTO THEEE?!
YA' EVER HAVE ONE OF THOSE DAYS?

FROM OUT OF NOWHERE...
BUT MOST LIKELY SOMEWHERE...
RUN FROD!!! WE'VE GOTCHA COVERED.
AN UNEXPECTED BONUS ROUND!
OUCH!!! WATCH THE SHRUBERY!!

THERE'S NO PLACE LIKE HOME! THERE'S NO PLACE LIKE HOME!
WHERE'S A RED, RUBY FLOWER POT WHEN YOU NEED ONE?!
BING!
BING!
COME ON FRED. HURRY

THE BOOGIMAN, TOOTHFAIRY AND CUPID COMBINED ARE NO MATCH FOR THE HOLY GO-HOST !!!
GET OFF'A MY WING YOU DIVINE MR. KOTTER LOOK-A-LIKE!
ZING!!!
OHMMMWW

COME HERE YOU
HUNKA, HUNKA
BURNIN' HEDGE!
I GUESS TWO IN THE HAND IS WORTH ONE IN THE HEDGE.
YO YO SUCKA WORD? SUBTITLE: WHAT THE HELL DOES THAT MEAN?
I HAVE NO CLUE.
FRED HAS ELUDED ME FOR THE MOMENT... BUT HIS FLUNKIES WILL MAKE A HEAVENLY APPETIZER!!!
WE'RE DOOMED!!! UNLESS... OUR ONLY CHANCE IS TO NAB A WORTHY HOSTAGE SO THAT WE CAN NEGOCIATE OUR WAY OUTTA THIS DILEMMA!
WHA' SUCKA?! SUBTITLE: BUT WHO?!
I'VE GOT IT!

BACK OFF, BIG GUY!... OR CHARLIE HESTON IS NO MOE!!!
TA-DAA!!!
NOOO!!! ANYONE BUT MOE!
SNAP OUT OF IT YOU IDIOTS AND HELP ME RESCUE MOSES!

WAIT A SEC!
WHERE ARE THE ARCHEOLOGISTS AND PAINTING?!
POP!!!
OH MYSELF!!! WE CAN'T WASTE ANYMORE TIME. WE'VE GOT TO RECOVER THAT PAINTING!
GONE!
YOW!!! RECOVER THAT PAINTING! DEFINETLY RECOVER THAT PAINTING!
PHEW!!! THAT WAS TOO CLOSE.
LOOKS LIKE THEY STIFFED YOU, MOSES.
BASTARDS!

rf
THE RICKI FAKE SHOW!!!!
COMING UP NEXT, ON TODAY'S SHOW... THINGS THAT COULDN'T POSSIBLY BE TRUE, BUT WE'LL TRY TO CONVINCE YOU ANYWAY!
WE HAVE PROOF THAT WILLY SHATNER'S HAIR IS REAL!... MIKEY JACKSON IS A NORMAL GUY!... AND IRREVOCABLE PROOF THAT JESUS WAS BLACK!... AND MUCH MORE AFTER THESE COMMERCIAL MESSAGES...
JUST CHECKING IN.
OK, ARE YOU GUYS CLEAR ON WHAT TO DO?
TELEPHONE
TELEPHONE
NO PROBLEM, BOSS.
EVERYTHING IS GOING ACCORDING TO PLAN.

AND NOW BACK TO OUR SHOW!
THE RICKI FAKE SHOW!!!
THE BIG GUY MUST HAVE HIS TOGA IN A KNOT RIGHT ABOUT NOW.
THAT SURE WOULD BE A SIGHT TO SEE! HEE HEE HEE!
ARE THE ROOMERS TRUE, MR. RANGER?
LOOK.. I SWING STRAIT... FIGHTING UP CLOSE AND PERSONAL WITH CROOKS, GROOMING MY HORSE IN PRIVATE AND SPENDING QUALITY TIME WITH MY KIMOSOBI JUST TAKES UP ALL OF MY TIME.
WELL FOLKS... THERE YOU HAVE IT.
NEXT, WE WILL TAKE A LOOK AT ST. PETE'S LONG, LOST PORTRAIT OF A BLACK JESUS

FILMING THE RICKI FAKE SHOW ON SET #666
20TH CENTURY SUX.
I'M SORRY, BUT I CAN'T LET YOU IN... THE STUDIO IS FULL.
YOU DON'T UNDERSTAND, I AM...

NOW I THINK THAT YOU DON'T UNDERSTAND! IT WOULD TAKE AN ACT OF GOD TO GET YOU INSI...
SNAP!!!

J. DENVERMOBILE
IMMINENT CRASH!!!

BOOM!!!
FOR 500 POINTS!... WHO IS THE MOST WRATHFUL GOD THAT YOU KNOW?
YOU'RE KINDA TESTY FOR A DIVINE BEING, AREN'T YOU?
QUICK!!! THERE'S NO TIME TO WASTE!

WE ARE NOW GOING TO UNVAIL THE PAINTING THAT YOU HAVE ALL BEEN WAITING FOR!
CARBON DATED BEYOND A SHADOW OF A DOUBT AUTHENTIC, IRREVOCABLE PROOF THAT *JESUS WAS BLACK!!!*

GOOD GOLLY!
TUTTI FRUITY!
WHAMP BOMP ALOO BOP!
HE ALWAYS SAID THAT HE WAS THE *TRUE KING!*

OK GUYS, DO YOUR STUFF.
GRAND FAIRY
I ♥ ED MURPHY
THIS IS BLASPHEMY!!! JESUS WAS A WHITEY!!!
BLACK TRUTH!!! WHITE LIES!!! YOU WHITE BREAD, JIVE TURKEY, SUCKA!!!
MY PRODUCER WAS RIGHT... TODAY'S THEME IS POTENTIALLY DANGEROUS. I KNEW THAT I SHOULD HAVE WENT WITH BIKER FLOOZIES WITH UZIES OR GAY, STRAIT, FAT, SKINNY DOCTORS... GULP!!!
WE'RE TOO LATE!
YA! WE'RE TOO LATE! DEFINETLY TOO LATE!

WHATTA SCORE!!!
HA! HA! HA! HA! HA!
RACIST MOTHA
$!!@#¢%
SPIKED
LEE
PREJUDICE
!#¢$@*!
NH
HELL
D.
CBERRY

SOMEWHERE IN, HEAVEN...
PAY UP ABE... I WIN.
YA GOT ME, MR. KING... I DIDN'T THINK THAT THE LITTLE FLOWER COULD PULL THIS OFF.
I DID HOWEVER ENJOY IT WHEN RICKI FAKE GOT GERALDO'D IN THE FACE WITH A FOLD-AWAY CHAIR.
YA.. I ENJOYED THAT TOO.
I HAD A DREAM.
THE GOD DAMN END!

HAPPY NICK'S

FRED the POSSESSED FLOWER

"MR. NOTHINGFACE"

GUEST STARRING:
GOD & SATAN

HAPPY NICK'S
FRED
THE POSSESSED
FLOWER
"MR. NOTHINGFACE"
DREAMING HEAVENLY COMMERCIALS,
BUT AWAKING TO HELL ON EARTH.
TANGIBLE LIMITATIONS,
EVER SINCE BIRTH.
LIFE SOUNDS INSPIRING,
CHALLENGING AND GLORIOUS.
BUT MORE OFTEN THEN NOT,
TEDIOUS AND LABORIOUS.
IF ONLY IMAGINATION AND REALITY,
COULD MERGE INTO ONE.
HARMLESS AND PLAYFUL SIN AFTER SIN,
DAMN THAT WOULD BE FUN.
RIVER STYX...
REFRESHING!

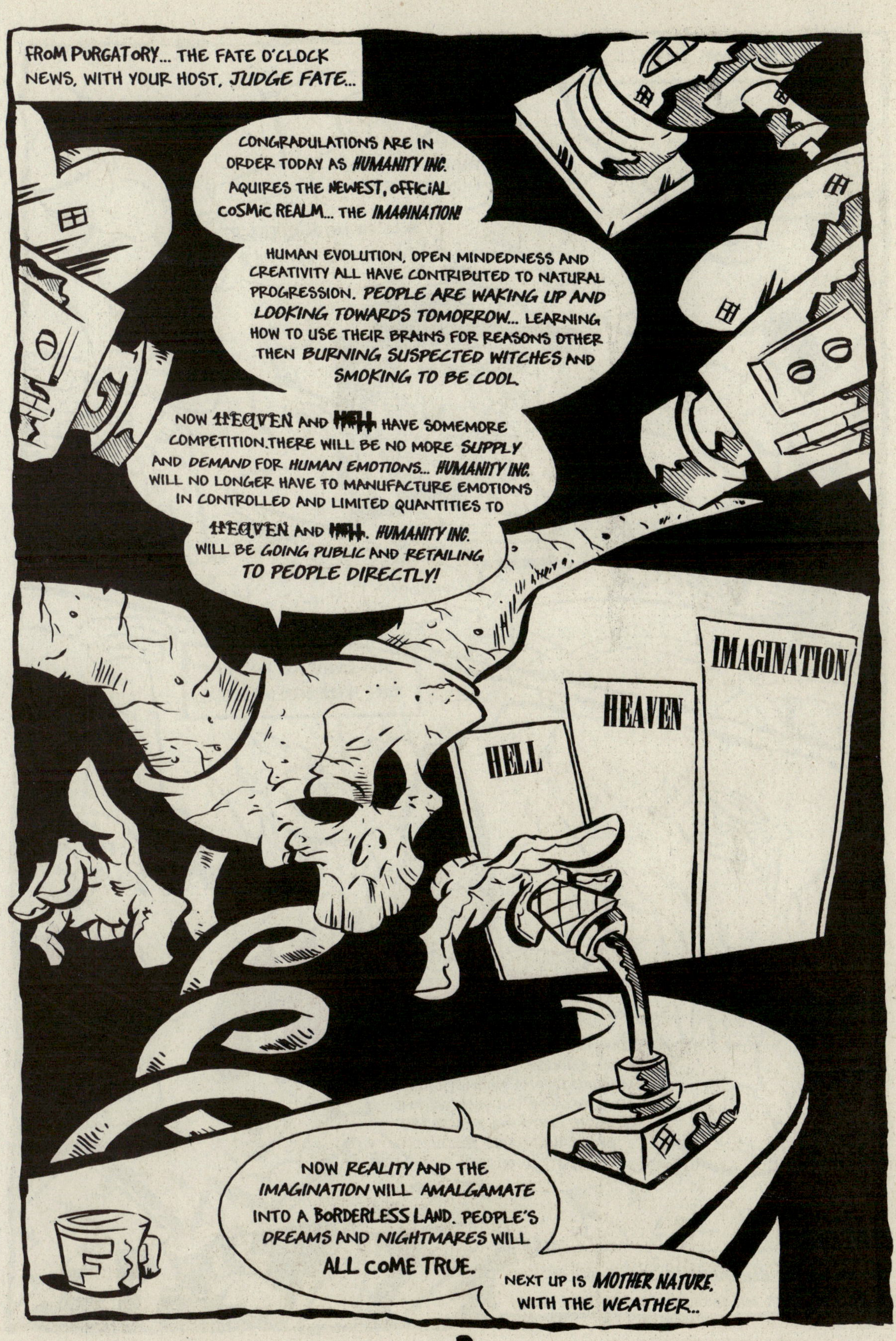

FROM PURGATORY... THE FATE O'CLOCK NEWS, WITH YOUR HOST, JUDGE FATE...
CONGRADULATIONS ARE IN ORDER TODAY AS HUMANITY INC. AQUIRES THE NEWEST, OFFICIAL COSMIC REALM... THE IMAGINATION!
HUMAN EVOLUTION, OPEN MINDEDNESS AND CREATIVITY ALL HAVE CONTRIBUTED TO NATURAL PROGRESSION. PEOPLE ARE WAKING UP AND LOOKING TOWARDS TOMORROW... LEARNING HOW TO USE THEIR BRAINS FOR REASONS OTHER THEN BURNING SUSPECTED WITCHES AND SMOKING TO BE COOL.
NOW HEAVEN AND HELL HAVE SOMEMORE COMPETITION. THERE WILL BE NO MORE SUPPLY AND DEMAND FOR HUMAN EMOTIONS... HUMANITY INC. WILL NO LONGER HAVE TO MANUFACTURE EMOTIONS IN CONTROLLED AND LIMITED QUANTITIES TO HEAVEN AND HELL. HUMANITY INC. WILL BE GOING PUBLIC AND RETAILING TO PEOPLE DIRECTLY!
IMAGINATION
HEAVEN
HELL
NOW REALITY AND THE IMAGINATION WILL AMALGAMATE INTO A BORDERLESS LAND. PEOPLE'S DREAMS AND NIGHTMARES WILL ALL COME TRUE.
NEXT UP IS MOTHER NATURE, WITH THE WEATHER...
F

LUCIFER'S LIVINGROOM, IN HELL...
THERE GOES THE NEIGHBOURHOOD.
WELL DIP ME IN SCHERBERT AND CALL ME CHILI!
PARDON?
SOMEWHERE IN THAT BIG CASBAR IN THE SKY...
HAVING HELL AS COMPETITION IS BAD ENOUGH! I KNOW THAT THE IMAGINATION IS AN INEVIDABLE SIDE-EFFECT OF THE POSITIVE AND NEGATIVE EMOTIONS PURCHASED BY HEAVEN AND HELL... BUT, COME ON?
DITTO!
NOW WITH HUMANITY INC. GOING RETAIL, REALITY ISN'T BIG ENOUGH FOR THE THREE OF US!

AT THE COSMIC INTERSECTION OF OFFICIAL BELIEFS... OTHERWISE KNOWN AS THE LIMBO ROOM...
HUMANITY INC. IMAGINATION
HEAVEN
REALITY
THE TOMMY SNYDER SHOW SUBSIDIARY OF HELL
FATE DEPT. PURGATORY
THE MAKERS OF MIND GAMES
HELL
HELL
FOR OUR OWN WELL BEING AND THE SAKE OF HUMAN LIMITATIONS AS WE KNOW THEM, ACTION MUST BE TAKEN!!!
I KNOW THAT HELL IS ALITTLE DUBIOUS AND HEAVEN IS ALITTLE RIGHTEOUS, BUT HUMANITY INC!... THEY'RE SO SICK AND TWISTED, IT'S NOT FUNNY. IT'S BEYOND COMPREHENSION WHAT WILL HAPPEN IF JUDGE FATE ALLOWS HUMANITY INC. TO RUN RAMPANT OVER LIFE ON EARTH!
I HAVEN'T EVEN MENTIONED HUMANITY INC.'S PRESIDENT. HE'S A REAL WINGNUT!

THEY CALL ME MR. NOTHINGFACE!!! I'M THE SOLE STOCK HOLDER OF A CRAZY PLACE!
HUMANITY INC. IS THE RETAIL NAME! IMAGINATION IS THE PERVERBIAL GAME!
TO WREAK EMOTIONAL HAVOC IS WHAT I LIKE! NO PERSON IS SAFE, NOT TINA, NOT IKE!
ALL DREAMS AND NIGHTMARES ARE SOON TO COME TRUE! FOR ALL OF FRED'S READERS, ESPECIALLY YOU!!!

INFILTRATING THE HUMAN BRAIN, THOUGHTS FULFILLED AND GOALS INSANE!
METRE MAIDS AND PAPER CUTS, EUROPEAN MEN WITH HAIRLESS BUTTS!
PARKI INFRAC
FREE
FREE
FREE
EXOTIC CARS ON THE HOUSE... LEGALLY COMMIT YOUR ANNOYING SPOUSE!
LOONEY BIN

TO HECK WITH MONOGAMY, DON'T BE NERVOUS!
3... 2... 1...
EAT ME IN ST. LOUIS
DRIVE-THRU
MENU
PAY BACK TIME, FOR BOTCHED DRIVE-THRU SERICE!
EXIT

BACK IN HELL...
IF WE DON'T DO SOMETHING ABOUT MR. NOTHINGFACE SOON, I PREDICT BIG PROBLEMS FOR HELL.
I THINK THAT HIS RHYMES ARE CATCHY! THERE REALLY, SKIDDLY WAA WAA!... MAN.
LOUIE, TRY TO FOLLOW ALONG FOR A SEC... WHEN A HUMAN BODY EXPIRES IT'S SOUL GOES TO EITHER HEAVEN OR HELL, RIGHT?
CORRECT-AMUNDO!!!
RIGHT... BUT, AS PEOPLE START BLENDING THEIR IMAGINATIONS WITH REALITY, THEY WILL BECOME INVINCIBLE... LET'S JUST SAY THAT IT COULD POTENTIALLY BE A COLD DAY IN HELL BEFORE WE COLLECT ANYMORE SOULS.
HELLS TO BETTSY!!! I DIDN'T THINK OF THAT!
SERIOUSLY?

IT GETS WORSE.
YER FREAKIN' ME OUT DUDE! I WANT MY BLANKY!
WELL, WE WON'T BE ABLE TO SELL ANYMORE PERSONAL CONTRACTS IN EXCHANGE FOR SOULS BECAUSE NOW PEOPLE CAN IMAGINE ANYTHING THAT THEY WANT.
WELL JUST STICK A FORK IN ME 'CAUSE MY UNHOLY ASS IS DONE!
DON'T GET YOUR HORNS ALL TWISTED. I'LL SEND THE BOYS TO ROUGH UP OUR FRIEND, MR. NOTHINGFACE. THAT SHOULD TEACH HIM NOT TO MESS WITH HELL.
GRETCHEN, CAN YOU GET MY FLUNKIES ON THE PHONE FOR ME?
RIGHT AWAY, MR. THE POSSESSED FLOWER.

OK, NOTHINGFACE...
AS OLIVIA USED TO SAY,
LET'S GET PHYSICAL!
AIN'T NUTTIN' TO IT, BUT TA DO IT, SUCKA MO FO!
WHAT MY TWO COMRADS ARE TRYING TO ARTICULATE IS THAT WE'RE GONNA KICK THE SASPIRILLA OUTTA YOU.
TOOTHFAIRY,
BOOGIMAN AND CUPID,
WHAT A SURPRISE! I'LL MAKE IT WORTH YOUR WHILE, IF YOU OVER LOOK MY DEMISE!

A PROMISCUOUS LAD, TOO YOUNG FOR KICKS! HOW ABOUT A GROWN UP APPEARANCE, SO THAT YOU CAN DATE ALL THE CHICKS!
SCARING PEOPLE, IS NOT YOU BY FAR! YOUR DESIRED CAREER, IS TO BE A PORNO STAR!
DRUNK JUICE
ENDLESS FOOTBALL AND BEER, IS WHAT YOU WOULD DIG! SO BE NICE TO ME, OR YOU'LL GET JACK YOU FAT PIG!

CURSE THAT
MR. NOTHINGFACE!!!
GOOD IDEA, FRED! LET'S GO WITH THAT.
IT WAS JUST AN EXPRESSION.
AHHH?
I'D LIKE TO DROP THAT NO GOOD, NOTHINGFACE INTO A VAT OF BOILING HOT CHERRY PIE FILLING!!!
'CAUSE YOUR EVIL!
YUK! YUK! YUK!
SATANLY!!!
HELLO, MY NAME IS:
CURLZIBUB

MONEY ON TREES,
DOGS ON FLEAS!
NO MORE
DISEASE,
IMMORTALITY
PLEASE!

TWO FOR ONE SALES ON PANTS, LET'S GIVE PEACE A CHANCE!
THE DEMISE OF ZITS, DOUBLE D TI...

...TIMES UP, MR. NOTHINGFACE!!! I'M SICK'A EMOTIONS FLYING HIGH! TIME TO SETTLE THIS, MANNO E FLOWERO!
GET A GRIP FRED, I'M THE NEW FASHION! PLEASE, MR. POSSESSED FLOWER, HAVE SOME COMPASSION!
ZAP!!!
COMPASSION!!!
ZAP!!!
OK... I GUESS?

HELL'S SPA...
WHAT HAPPENED?
HE COLD COCKEDME WITH SOME COMPASSION... SNEEKY BASTARD.
GEEZ-UZ ANTI-CHRIST!!! WHAT'RE WE GONNA DO NOW?! BANKRUPCY, HERE WE COME!
HUMANITY INC. IS TOO POWERFUL RIGHT NOW TO STRONG ARM. NOTHINGFACE HAS EVERYBODY DAY DREAM BELIEVING... WE'VE GOTTA OUT SMART HIM, IT'S OUR ONLY CHANCE IN HELL... LITERALLY!
SO WHAT YOU'RE SAYING IS THAT IT'S HOPELESS!!!
MAYBE FOR YOU. BUT NOT FOR... WAIT A SECOND, THAT'S IT!!!

WHAT?
HOPELESS?!
HOPELESS! HELPLESS! HELL-LESS!!!
LOUIE, I NEED YOU TO ARRANGE A MEETING WITH HEAVEN, ASAP !!!
THAT'S IT, WE'RE TOAST! KA-PUT! FREAKIN' FINEE'! PARDON MY FRENCH.
A-G
M
N-S
NOT QUITE... IT'S TIME TO SHOW MR. NOTHINGFACE JUST WHO'S THE MEANEST FLOWER IN THE GARDEN!

BUSINESS IS BOOMING, EMOTIONS ARE ZOOMING!
BANK
UNPUNISHED CRIMES, DEATH TO ALL MIMES!
NO MORE LEGAL AGE FOR BOOZE,
AND FOR NO REASON, DANCING KANGAROOS!!!

DEEP IN THE HEART OF DOWNTOWN HEAVEN...
HOLY SMOKES CIGAR CO.
HOLY SPIRITS DISTILLERY
HOLY TOLEDO HALO REPAIR
MIKE'S SPORT SANDLES & TOGAS FACTORY OUTLET
I HAVE A SOLUTION TO A MUTAL PROBLEM OF OURS... KNOWN AS HUMANITY INC.
GO ON...

THE UNHOLIEST DISTRICT IN TOWN...
INDIVIDUALLY, HEAVEN AND HELL DON'T GENERATE ENOUGH REVENUE TO PURCHASE A LARGE ENOUGH EMOTIONAL ORDER OF IMPATIENCE, BOREDUM AND CLOSED MINDEDNESS TO PUT A DAMPER ON THE IMAGINATION. BUT, IF WE WORK TOGETHER, WE COULD BUY ENOUGH NEGATIVE EMOTION AND HOPELESS IGNORANCE TO DESTROY THE IMAGINATION FOR GOOD!
WE'LL USE HUMANITY INC.'S OWN EMOTIONS AGAINST THEM! WE'LL TRICK NOTHINGFACE WITH ONE OF HIS OWN PRECIOUS, LITTLE, HUMAN EMOTIONS, GREED!!!
HE'LL NEVER KNOW WHAT HIT HIM UNTIL IT'S TOO LATE!
YOU ARE FORGETTING THAT IT IS COSMICALLY ILLEGAL FOR HEAVEN AND HELL TO COLLABORATE ON ANY BUSINESS VENTURES.

THE BIG GUY'S RIGHT, FRED! IF JUDGE FATE FINDS OUT THAT WE'RE ALL IN KAHOOTS, HE'LL SHUT US DOWN AND LOCK US UP!
AND I HEAR THAT THE HOLDING SELLS IN PURGATORY ARE WORST THEN CELLIBACY!
AMEN!!!
I WON'T TELL IF YOU GUYS WON'T!
FROD, ARE YOU NUTS?! I CAN'T WORK WITH THIS BIBLE THUMPER!
BITE ME, YOU SATANIC SIMPLETON!
UMMM?

WE CAN ORDER ALL OF THE STUBBORNNESS, VANITY AND EGO THAT OUR HEARTS DESIRE. AFTER WE RE-PRIVATIZE HUMANITY INC.
OKW...
OKW...
GOOD... NOW WHAT WE HAVE TO DO IS SUMMON ALL OF HEAVEN AND HELL'S STOCK BROKERS AND GET THEM TO BUY EVERY LAST IGNORANT SHARE OF HUMAN EMOTION FROM HUMANITY INC.
AND FOR OUR OWN PRECAUTIONS, LET'S KEEP THIS HUSH-HUSH!

THE CELESTIAL STOCK EXCHANGE...
BOREDUM
HATE
JEALOUSY
ANGER
GREED
LUST
LAZINESS
STUBBORNNESS
IGNORANCE
MINDGAMES
IF YOUR FRIENDS JUMPED OFF OF A BRIDGE, WOULD YOU?
LOVE
BUY!!!
SELL!!!
BUY!!!
SELL!!!
BUY!!!
SELL!!!

YES, I'D LIKE TO PURCHASE ALL OF YOUR AVAILABLE SHARES IN EVERY *IGNORANT EMOTION* THAT YOU'VE GOT!...
THAT BIG STOCK EXCHANGE IN THE SKY.
WORK IS HELL!
THAT'S RIGHT, ALL OF THE *IGNORANCE* YOU'VE GOT, BABY!
BUY!!! BUY!!! BUY!!!

I'M EMOTIONALLY RICH, THIS MUCH IS TRUE! THE EARTH IS BEING SHOWERED IN IGNORANCE, COURTESY OF THE BIG GUY AND LOU!
THE BUSINESS THAT THEY'VE GIVEN ME, IS REALLY QUITE SWELL! THOSE STOCK BROKERS FROM HEAVEN, AND THOSE STOCK BROCKERS FROM HELL!
IGNORANCE!!!
I HAVE A BAD FEELING, I'M SENSING BAD THINGS!
WHAT'S UP WITH THOSE HORNS, AND WHAT'S UP WITH THOSE WINGS?!

WAIT JUST A SEC, SOMETHING ISN'T RIGHT! WHERE'S MY IMAGINATION, IT'S NOWHERE IN SIGHT?!
I'VE BEEN TRICKED, THAT'S JUST MY LUCK! ONE LAST APPROPRIATE WORD, THAT WORD IS FFFW...

...FROD!!! EXCELLENT WORK! MR. NOTHINGFACE AND THE IMAGINATION ARE BANKRUPT... RESTORING PEOPLE TO THE MINDLESS CATTLE THAT THEY SHOULD BE!
AMEN!!!
TO BE CONTINUED, IN HELL?

HAPPY PREDATOR PUBLICATIONS
HAPPY NICK'S
FRED the POSSESSED FLOWER
10
"THE AGNOSTIC ODD COUPLE"
FOR HEAVEN'S SAKE!!!
AHHH HELL!!!
THE SEQUEL TO "MR. NOTHINGFACE"...
GUEST STARRING: GOD & SATAN

THE SEQUEL TO "MR. NOTHINGFACE"...
"THE AGNOSTIC ODD COUPLE"
IN EVERY BIT OF GOOD, THERE IS ALWAYS ALITTLE BIT OF EVIL AND VISE VERSA, WE CAN PUT A MAN ON THE MOON, AS THE DIVORCE RATE CLIMBS. CHOLESTEROL GOODIES GO HAND IN HAND WITH SUPERFICIAL STANDARDS. LIKE PEOPLE AND PLANTS WITH OXYGEN AND CARBONDIOXIDE, SOMETHING NEEDS TO BREATH GOOD JUST AS SOMETHING NEEDS TO BREATH EVIL, IN ORDER TO EXIST. AND FOR US TO MOVE FORWARD, WE NEED TO WEAR A SEE-THRU BLIND FOLD... WHAT?

CHEERS, GENTLEMEN !!!
TO OUR SUCCESS IN GETTING
RID OF HUMANITY INC!!!
RIGHT ON,
SUCKA!
HERE, HERE!
AMEN!!!
FRED
the POSSESSED
FLOWER
Creator
Writer
Illustrator
HAPPY
NICK

EVERYBODY FREEZE!!!
WE'RE THE FBI!!! FATES BUREAU OF INVESTIGATIONS!
WHAT THE?!...

WHAT IN THE HEAVENS
IS GOING ON HERE?!
YOU GENTLEMEN ARE UNDER ARREST FOR WORKING TOGETHER AND ACCOMPLISHING SOMETHING USEFUL. YOU HAVE THE RIGHT TO SHUT UP, IF YOU CANNOT SHUT UP, WE WILL SHUT YOU UP.
AT LEAST YOU GUYS AREN'T AS HARSH AS STATE TROOPERS.

JUDGE FATES COURTROOM, SOMEWHERE IN PURGATORY...
WILL THE DEFENDANTS RISE...
YOU ARE ALL CHARGED WITH BEING CO-OPERATIVE. HOW DO YOU PLEAD?
LIKE THIS... PLEASE!!! PLEASE!!! DON'T SEND ME TO PURGATRAZ!!! PLEASE!!! DON'T LET THE BAD MAN HURT ME!
AGNAUSEA FILLS THE ROOM...
THE JURY WILL IGNORE THAT LAST COMMENT.
100% OJ

THE BIG GUY FORCED ME TO BUY ALL OF THE IGNORANT STOCKS AVAILABLE. I EVEN SAW HIM AND LUCIFER SHAKE... UHHH?... HAND AND TENTACLE.
YES, HEAVEN AND HELL'S EXECUTIVES HIRED ME TO BUY UP ALL OF THE USELESS STOCKS I COULD, FROM HUMANITY INC. THEY ACTUALLY PUT ASIDE THEIR DIFFERENCES TO WORK TOGETHER... LET THE BASTARDS FRY!!!
A FEW MINUTES AND A COUPLE OF ROLLS OF RED TAPE LATER...
THE JURY HAS ARRIVED AT A VERDICT.
GASP!!!
UHHH!!!
GULP!!!
UMMM!!!
BURP!!!

GUILTY!!!
GUILTY!!! GUILTY!!!
CAN'T WE ALL JUST GET ALONG! THE GLOVE WASN'T MINE! MY DOG MADE ME DO IT! TEMPORARY INSANITY! SOCIETY FORCED ME!
?!
DUMB ASS!
IMBECILE!
WHERE THE HELL IS COCKRAN!!! I DID HIM A HUGE FAVOR! HE OWES ME BIG TIME!

FATE'S PRIVATE CHAMBER...
IN ORDER TO PROTECT YOU TWO BRAVE STOOL PIGEONS, WE HEREAT PURGATORY HAVE DECIDED TO PUT YOU INTO THE CELESTIAL WITNESS RELOCATION PROGRAM.
WHAAA?...
THE FLOWER WILL UNDOUBTEDLY ATTEMPT TO HAVE THE BOTH OF YOU ASSASINATED... REMEMBER THE SONNY BONO THING?
SINCE PURGATORY'S BUDGET HAS UNFORTUNATLEY BEEN CUT BACK, WE CAN'T AFFORD SEPARATE IDENTITIES FOR BOTH OF YOU... SO YOU'LL BE COSMIC ROOMMATES, SO TO SPEAK.
YOU DO, HOWEVER HAVE A FEW CHOICES AS TO YOUR NEW IDENTITIES...
YOU CAN BE MR. AND MRS. STRANDED FAMILY ROBINSON... A COUPLE OF GRAZING CATTLE OR A PAIR OF OVERLY POLITE, BEER SWILLING, HOCKEY FANS FROM CANADA..

CELESTIAL PRISON BREAK... FROM PURGATRAZ...
DAMN, THE ALARM WENT OFF! HEY, WHERE THE HELL IS LOUIE?!
ALARM!!! ALARM!!!
I DUNNO?
?!
FREEZE, YOU SNEAKY, LITTLE DEVIL!
DAMN YOU TWO-SCOOPS A'RAISINS!!! YOU DO THIS TO ME EVERY SINGLE TIME!
2 SCOOPS

WELCOME TO YOUR NEW APARTEMENT GENTLEMEN.
WOW!!! TAX FUNDED FREE STUFF! LET'S ABUSE OUR PRESENT SITUATION TO THE FULLEST OF OUR ABILITIES... I'LL GET THE HONOR BAR, YOU SWIPE THE TOWELS!
THIS ISN'T A HOTEL, THIS IS OUR APARTMENT, YOU DEMONIC DUMMY!
NOT PAID FOR BY INNOCENT TAX PAYERS?
NOPE...

AWW
CRUDMUFFINS!!! I ALREADY DRANK EVERYTHING IN THE HONOR BAR!
MR. CLEANLY
JOHONEX
THOSE AREN'T HONOR BAR DRINKS, YOU SINNFUL SIMPLETON. THEY ARE HOUSE HOLD CLEANING PRODUCTS.
YA MEAN TA'TELL ME THAT TOILET DUCK ISN'T AN IMPORTED BRAND'O WHISKY?
THAT WOULD EXPLAIN WHY IT DIDN'T MIX VERY WELL WITH TONIC WATER.. BURP!!!
THUD!!!
TOILET DUCK

LATER...
WELCOME BACK TO THE MULTI-RELIGIOUS SHOPPING NETWORK... MY SOCKS ARE HOLY...
REALLY. MY SOCKS ARE SATANIC!
HEY ANGEL FACE, YA'WANNA GO OUT AND SIN SOMEWHERE TONITE?
NO. AND COULD YOU GET YOUR FILTHY, EVIL FEET OFF OF THE COFFEE TABLE, PLEASE!!!
RRRRR!!! FFFFT!!! FFFFT!!! YOU'RE UNAPPRECIATED, YOU'RE GRUMPY, YOU'RE TIRED... BUT YOU'RE HAVING ONE HELL OF A GOOD HAIR DAY!
THANK YOU.

¡SLAVE ALL DAY LONG, KEEPING THIS APARTEMENT CLEAN!
NOT TO MENTION COOKING ALL OF YOUR MEALS!
?!
I'M ONLY GOING TO LIVE HERE UNTIL I CAN SAVE UP ENOUGH MONEY TO BUY MYSELF MY OWN IDENTITY, YOU KNOW!
YOU'LL MISS ME WHEN I'M GONE!
WE GOTTA TAKE SOME STARCH OUTTA YOUR FIG LEAF, MAN. I TELL'YA WHAT... LET'S GO OUT TONITE AND PICK UP SOME CHICK-BABES!

PURGATRAZ... CELL BLOCK 666...
OK, THE COAST IS CLEAR.
DAMN PLASTIC, NOVELTY SHOVEL BUSTED!
IT'S OK! WE'RE THROUGH!
SWEET!

LOOK AT THE SEXY MENZ!
HEAVENLY!
DELICIOUS! I'M A VEGETARIAN, SO I GOT DIBS ON THE FLOWER!

PUT IT BACK!
PUT IT BACK!
BIG GUY, PLUG THE FREAKIN' HOLE!
ZAP!!!
FIRE IN THE HOLE!
PHEW!

A TYPICAL CANADIAN PUB...
EH!!!
THE LAND OF BEER...
EXIT
I AM
EH!!!
EH?!
EH!!!
EH?!
EH?!
GET ME AND MY FRIEND HERE A COUPLE'A SHOTS OF HELLFIRE WHISKY!
I DON'T DRINK.
NOT EVEN SOME HOLY SPIRITS? HEE! HEE! OK, OK... HE'LL HAVE A SHIRLEY TEMPLE...
MIX IT ONE PART SHIRLEY, TWO PARTS TEQUILA

SO I SAID TO THE WISE MAN, BUDDY... YA'THINK YER SO DAMN...
BURP!!!
CANADIANS...
EH!!!
EH!!!
EH?!
HEY, HEY! LOOKEE THAR! CHICKS AHOY!
THUMP!!!
SO'S I SAID...
EH!!!
HEY?... WHAT IN THE HEAVENS GOIN' ON HERE?

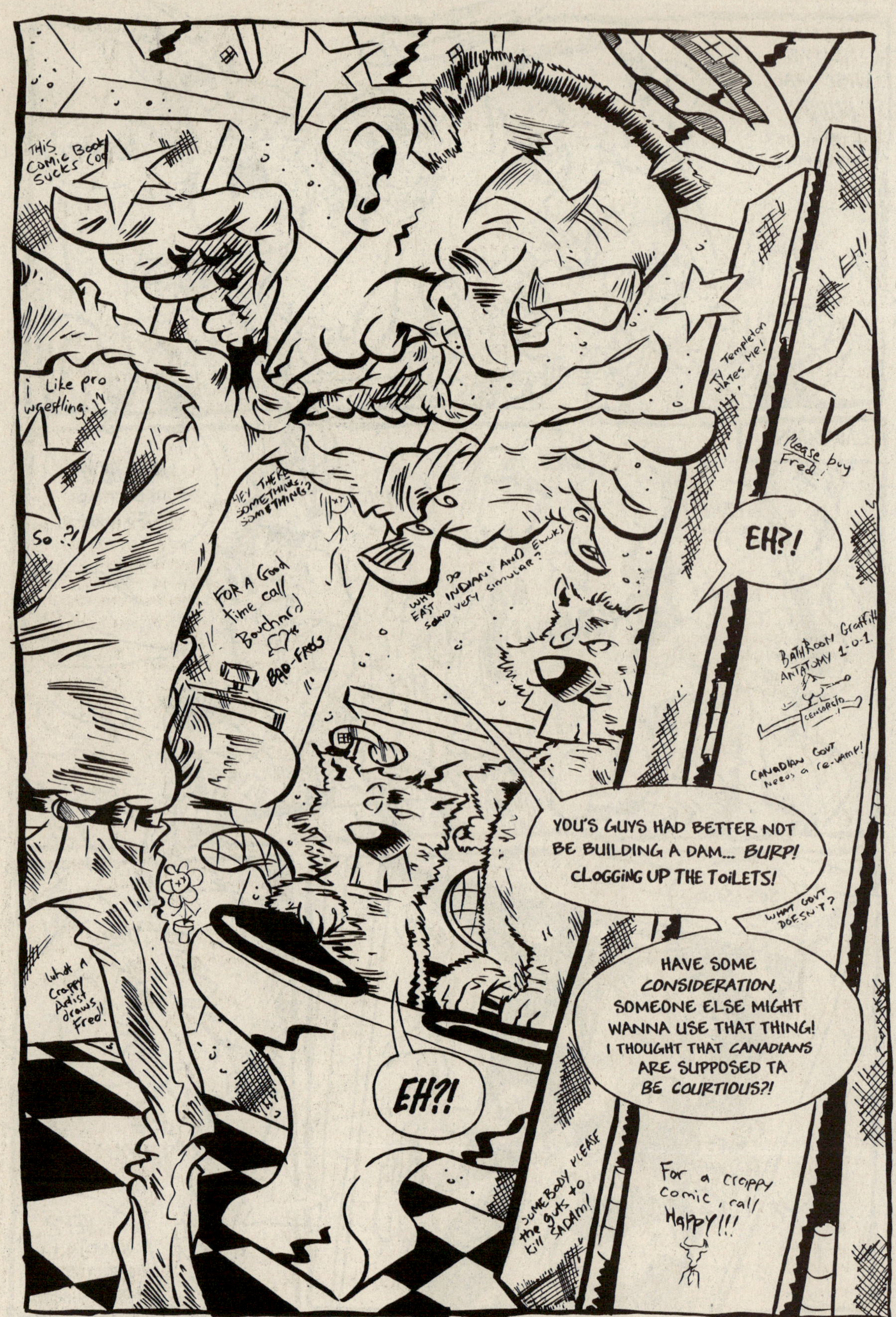

THIS Comic Book Sucks Coo
i Like pro wrestling.
So ?!
FOR A Good time call Bouchard
BAD-FROGS
WHY DO EAST INDIANS AND EWOKS SOUND VERY SIMULAR?
Ty Templeton Hates Me!
EH!
Please buy Fred!
EH?!
BATHROOM Graffiti ANATOMY 1-0-1.
CENSORED
CANADIAN GOVT NEEDS a RE-VAMP!
YOU'S GUYS HAD BETTER NOT BE BUILDING A DAM... BURP! CLOGGING UP THE TOILETS!
WHAT GOVT DOESN'T?
HAVE SOME CONSIDERATION, SOMEONE ELSE MIGHT WANNA USE THAT THING! I THOUGHT THAT CANADIANS ARE SUPPOSED TA BE COURTIOUS?!
What A Crappy Artist draws Fred!
EH?!
SOMEBODY PLEASE the guts to kill SADAM!
For a crappy comic, call HAPPY!!!

OOOHH, I HAVE SUCH A HEAD ACHE.
GOOD MORNIN' ANGEL FACE!
EH!!!
EH!!!
YOU DIDN'T?!
DIDN'T WHAT?! DIDN'T PUT THE CAP ON THE TOOTHPASTE? DIDN'T PUT DOWN THE TOILET SEAT? DIDN'T GRADUATE FROM SENIOR KINDERGARDEN? DIDN'T VOTE CLINTON? WHAT IS IT?! SPIT IT OUT, MAN!!!
YOU DIDN'T, UMMM?... YOU KNOW?...
...GIVE THEM A FREE TOUR OF THE APARTEMENT?! YUP! THE GRAND TOUR, IF YA'KNOW WHAT I'M SAYIN?
I'M MOVING OUT! I CAN'T TAKE THIS!!!

FREE AT LAST!
FREE AT LAST!
PURGATRAZ!!!
LLLLEEEETTT MYYY PEEEOPLE GOOO!!!
I CAN'T BELIEVE THAT WE FINALLY ESCAPED. FROD, HOW DID YOU MANAGE TO DISTRACT EVERY GUARD AT THE SAME TIME AND LONG ENOUGH FOR US TO JUST WALK OUT OF THE FRONT DOORS?!
I HAVE FRIENDS IN LOW PLACES.

PURGATRAZ!
FRESH DONUTS'N COFFEE!!!
ME FiRST!
BRAND
X
HURRY UP, WILL'YA!
DONUTS 'N COFFEE!
JELLY FILLED!... HERE i COME, BABY!

NOW GENTLEMEN, I SUGGEST THAT WE TAKE CARE OF THOSE TWO INFORMANT STOCK BROKERS.
WHAT DO YOU WANT TO DO TO THEM, FRED? WHAT IF WE HANG THEM UP SIDE DOWN BY THEIR TOE NAILS AND HAVE AN ENGLISH SPECIAL AGENT WHIP THEM WITH BAMBOO REEDS, FOR THE REST OF ETERNITY?!
THE NAME'S BONDAGE... JAMES BONDAGE.
I HAVE AN EVEN MORE TERRIBLE IDEA! WHAT DO YOU SAY, WE FORGIVE THEM?!
WHAT KINDA DING BAT-WHACK JOB, ARE YOU?!
WHAT?

HOW ARE WE GOING TO FIND THEM?
i HAVE MY WAYS!
HA!!! HA!!! HA!!! HA!!! HA!!! HA!!! HA!!! HA!!! HA!!!
ABNORMALLY EVIL LAUGHTER!!!
The HELL PAGES
UNLISTED NUMBERS ONLY. CELESTIAL WITNESS RELOCATION PROGRAM RESIDENTS... HERE WE ARE...
I TRADED ONE OF THE PURGATRAZ GUARDS AN iLLEGAL COPY OF THE PAM AND TOMMY ViDEO IN EXCHANGE FOR THIS HANDY, LITTLE BOOK.
BRILLIANT HOLMES!
ELEMENTARY, MY DEAR SATAN.
NOW, LET'S GET THOSE BAS...

... KETBALL, ANYONE?
WHAT?
COME ON... WE'LL GO AND PLAY SOME BASKETBALL. IT'S GOOD FOR THE BODY AND THE SOUL TO GET SOME EXERCISE!
I WOULD, BUT JERRY STINKER IS ON TV. I PRACTICALLY MADE THIS GUY... HE WAS MY SENIOR YEAR PROJECT WHEN I WAS ATTENDING TEMPTATION SCHOOL!
TODAY ON THE JERRY STINKER SHOW WE'LL BE TALKING TO ANOTHER MESSED UP GROUP OF TRAILOR TRASH THAT HAVE NO HOPE OF EVER BEING SKINNY, RICH, SUCCESSFUL OR WORTH MORE THEN THE JUICE FOUND AT THE BOTTOM OF A CAN OF SPAM.
HE MARRIED MY THREE LEGGED NEICE'S POOLMAN!
SHE'S A LYING HO, JERRY!

DING!!!
DONG!!!
SUIT YOURSELF. BLASPHEMING BAS... EEERR?
MORNIN' SUNSHINE. MIND IF WE COME IN?

SO, ARE YOU TWO LOVE BIRDS GETTING ALONG ALRIGHT?
YOU DO REMEMBER MY COLLEAGUES LUCIFER, TOOTHFAIRY, BOOGIMAN AND CUPID?
GULP!!!
YO YO, SUCKA FOOS... WHAZUP WIT ALLADAT WHACK SPACE UP IN YO CRIB?!
SUBTITLE: HEY, LOOK AT ALL OF THE WASTED SPACE AT THE BOTTOM OF THIS DOUBLE PAGE SPREAD!!!

BURNIN'! BURNIN'!! BURNIN'!!! I WAS BURNIN' IN A RING'O FIRE!
Booo!!!
GASP!!!
THE BOOGIMAN IS RIGHT... THERE IS A TONE OF WASTED SPACE AT THE BOTTOM OF THIS DOUBLE PAGE SPREAD. BUT DON'T WORRY, I'LL FILL IT UP WITH SOME RELEVANT DIALOGUE. DIE!!! DIE!!! DIE!!! DIE!!! DIE!!! DIE!!! DIE!!! DIE!!! DIE!!! DIE!!! DIE!!! DIE!!! DIE!!! DIE!!!

EXHALE MAN! IT'S GONNA BE OK.
GAWK!!!
CHOKE!!!
DO YOU GUYS LIKE TACO'S?! 'CAUSE YOU'RE TOMMORROW'S SPECIAL! I'LL TAKE MY DEAD STOOL PIGEON WITH SOME NACHOS, PLEASE!!!
WHAT I HAVE HERE GENTLEMEN, IS A CONTRACT. A BRILLIANT CONTRACT, A WICKED CONTRACT, A BRILLIANTLY WICKED CONTRACT.
NOW WHAT WE ARE GOING TO DO, IS THE FOLLOWING... YOU TWO SWEETHEARTS ARE GOING TO TELL JUGDE FATE THAT YOU BOTH LIED ON THE STAND AND THAT HEAVEN AND HELL HAVE NEVER COLABORATED ON ANY BUSINESS ENDEAVORS... GET IT?
SURE... YOU'LL BOTH GO TO JAIL FOR PUGERY, BUT THAT WAY YOU GUYS WON'T HAVE TO LIVE TOGETHER ANYMORE. SO WHAT DO YOU SAY?

THAT'S cRAZY!
WHY WOULD I...
SERIOUSLY?
ZAP!!!
HEY, i'LL SiGN ANYTHiNG THAT MEANS THAT I DON'T HAVE TO LIVE WITH HOWDY DOODY HERE!
SOUNDS GREAT.
THANK YOU GENTLEMEN, SEE YOU IN HELL.
BY THE WAY, BIG GUY SAYS, Hi.

WELL, MY LITTLE BURNING HEDGE, WE CAN RELAX, FATE HAS PARDONED US. I'M SO GLAD THAT THINGS ARE BACK TO NORMAL.
ALMOST, BIG GUY... IT SEEMS THAT THE TEN COMANDMENTS HAVE BEEN UPDATED, SINCE WE WERE IN THE JOINT.
NUMBER ELEVEN... THOU SHALL USE THE BIG GUY'S POOL WHILE HE IS IN THE SLAMMER, FOR PARTIES AND DEBAUCHERY.
DO YOU KNOW HOW MANY SUB-RELIGIONS YOU'VE ACCIDENTALLY CREATED?! I WOULDN'T BE SURPRISED IF THE POPE TURNED CUBA CATHOLIC!
?!
OLA!
YEESH!!!

HOME SWEET HOME!
HEY, WHAT HAPPENED TO THE ANGEL AND THE DEMON AFTER THEY CONFESSED, ANYWAY? WHAT DID YOU DO WITH THEIR CONTRACT?
I LOVE YOU OFFICE, I LOVE YOU DESK, I LOVE YOU PHONE... AND I LOVE YOU, GRETCHEN!
?!
POOF!!!
WHAT CONTRACT?

WELL, I'M IN JAIL FOR THE REST OF MY UNNATURAL LIFE. BUT AT LEAST VIRTUE BOY WON'T BE ABLE TO KEEP ME FROM ENJOYING IT.
WELCOME TO YOUR NEW HOME, MEET YOUR CELLMATE.
NOOOOOOOOO!!!!!!!

NORMALLY, I HAVE SOME WITTY COMMENTARY FOR THE END OF EACH STORY... OR PERHAPS EVEN A SWIFT KICK IN THE COCONUTS OF COMEDY TO END OFF WITH. BUT FOR NOW...I'LL JUST SIT BACK AND LAUGH AT ALL OF YOU SILLY HUMANS, BECAUSE... HE WHO LAUGHS LAST, LAUGHS IN HELL!!!
HA!!!
HA!!!
HA!!!
HA!!!
HA!!!
HA!!!
THE END, FOR HEAVEN'S SAKE!!!

HAPPY PREDATOR PUBLICATIONS
HAPPY NICK'S
FRED the POSSESSED FLOWER
11
"COSMIC PENAL COLONY"
GO FISH.
GUEST STARRING: GOD & SATAN

FRED the POSSESSED FLOWER
"COSMIC PENAL COLONY"
THE TWENTIETH CENTURY IS JUST ANOTHER ROUND IN THE CELESTIAL BOXING MATCH BETWEEN THE POWERS OF THE DIVINE AND DAMNATION. THE TWENTIETH CENTURY WAS ALMOST A COMPLETE 10 AND 0 VICTORY FOR THE FORCES OF THE INFERNAL. HELL'S GREATEST VICTORIES WERE THE MASS PRODUCTION OF WARFARE, HOSTILITY, COMPETITIVENESS, INFOMERCIALS AND THE NEW VW BUG. THEN JUST AS THE WAR BETWEEN HEAVEN AND HELL SEEMED TO BE AT A CLOSE, A SUDDEN BLOW WAS STRUCK BY THE BIG GUY. THE MILLENIUM WAS NEAR AND HEAVEN WASN'T ABOUT TO GO DOWN WITHOUT A FIGHT.
YUM!!!
OUCHHH!!!
IS IT FATE? HEY, THAT'S ME!
Creator Writer Illustrator HAPPY NICK

THE SUPREME COURT OF THE UNITED GOVERNMENTS OF EARTH
ALL IN FAVOR?
AYE!!!
ALL OPPOSED?
THERE WAS A BRIEF PAUSE...
ALRIGHT THEN, IT HAS BEEN SETTLED... THE SUPREME COURT OF THE UNITED GOVERNMENTS OF EARTH HAVE AGREED THAT ANY AND ALL MEMBERS OF SOCIETY WILL BE EXCOMMUNICATED TO THE MOON IF THEY ARE DEEMED EVIL, OBSTRUCTIVE OR GENERALLY USELESS. ONCE THEY ARE PLACED INSIDE THE PENAL FACSILITIES LOCATED ON THE MOON THEY WILL HOPEFULLY CROAK.
CHEERS!!!
ALRIGHT!!!
I'LL DRINK TO THAT!

HELL'S FOYER...
TOOTHFAIRY, SWING BY PURGATORY AND PICK UP SOMEMORE UNREPENTANT DEADGUY APPLICATIONS.
WE'RE EXPECTING A HUGE SURGE OF REVENUE DUE TO THIS WHOLE MOON FIASCO.
WHAA?...
ARE THERE TWO L'S IN MILOSIVICH?
QUACK!!!
BEEP!!!
BEEP!!!
HELL'S PAGER

LUCiFER HERE, WHAT'S THE SCOOP?
HEY BOSS, THE BOOGIMAN AND I CONCUR THAT EVERYTHING IS GOING SMOOTHLY. ALL OF THE UNDESIRABLES ARE BEING LOADED INTO THE MOON SHUTTLES. THEY ALL SURE SEEM ANGRY AND BITTER..
NOT TO MENTION ALL OF THE GOVERNMENT CATS...MERCILESS AND SELFISH!
I WOULD HAVE BEEN TRUELY DANGEROUS IF I HAD ONLY SPENT A FEW MORE HOURS FILLING OUT "YES" ON ALL OF THOSE QUEBEC SEPARATION BALLOTS.
TO THE MOON, ALICE!!
MOON SHUTTLE LOADING DOCK.
Yo Yo!!! SUBTITLE: HELL IS GOING TO MAKE A KILLING!
I LOVE THE MOON!
WOODY
NEED... YOUNG... CHICKS...
SHUDDUP'N MOVE!

PURGATORY... FATE'S HEAD OFFICE...
RANDOM THOUGHT: IT'S STRANGE HOW WE ARE BAFFLED BY COMMON, DAILY OBSTACLES LIKE A CAR NOT STARTING OR REMOVING A CARPET STAIN...
BUT ALL OF THE SCI-FI MUMBO JUMBO THAT THEY TALK ABOUT ON STARTREK MAKES COMPLETE SENSE...
IN ORDER TO SUSTAIN LIFE SUPPORT WHILE THE MAIN DEFLECTORS ARE DOWN, CHANNEL ALL POWER FROM THE WARP CORE INTO THE DILYTHIUM CRYSTALS. SOUNDS ABOUT RIGHT TO ME.
ANOTHER RANDOM THOUGHT: IF EVERY GIRL ON THE PLANET LOOKED LIKE PAM ANDERSON... THERE WOULD BE NO TIME FOR SADNESS OR VIOLENCE...
BUT ON THE DOWN SIDE... IF EVERY GIRL LOOKED ALIKE THEY WOULD ALL JUST BE AVERAGE.

FATE'S MARKETING STRATEGIES AND PLANNING OFFICE
...
WHERE CAN I GET SOME APPLIC... HEY... WHADDA YOU GUYS HAVE ON THE DRAWING BOARD?
MOST OF FATE'S FILES ARE CLASSIFIED... WE CAN'T REALLY TELL YOU ANYTHING IMPORTANT. FOR EXAMPLE, WHAT'S GONNA HAPPEN ON THE NEXT SEASON OF FRIENDS.

HOW ABOUT SOMETHING INSIGNIFICANT?
OK.. THE PLANET EARTH IS GOING TO BE BLOWN UP! HEE!!! HEE!!!
WE CAN'T DIVULGE THE DETAILS AS TO HOW OR WHY BECAUSE THAT IS PRIVELEGDED INFORM...
?!
SMASH!!!
DIVULGE THIS!!!

DOWN BELLOW...
WHAT THE HELL IS GOING ON HERE?!
EXACTLY, BUT COULD YOU BE MORE SPECIFIC?
WHY IS HELL JUST GONNA SIT BACK AND LET THE EARTH GET DESTROYED?!
IT'S OUTTA MY LEAVES.

LOOK, TOOTH OLD BOY... THIS IS A HUMAN PROBLEM WHICH CAN ONLY BE SOLVED BY HUMAN HANDS...
NOT BY HEAVEN OR HELL.
THE HUMANS SHOULD AT LEAST BE WARNED SO THAT THEY CAN HAVE A FIGHTING CHANCE!
HEART BREAK MACHINE
LOOK WHAT HAPPENED WHEN WE DIDN'T WARN THEM ABOUT THE OZMONDS!
ENOUGH!!! NOW FORGET ABOUT IT BEFORE YOU UPSET SATAN!
?!

IN THE BIG CITY... SOMETIME DURING THE GREAT DEPRESSION...
FRANK!!!...
YOU AIN'T GOIN' ON LUNCH UNTIL YA FINISH ALL'DA SCAFFOLDING PREP!
#1 4MAN
I'M GREATLY DEPRESSED.

WHATTA CRAPPY LIFE...
WORKIN' MY BUTT OFF FOR PEANUTS... PEOPLE DRAGGIN' ME DOWN... THEY TELL ME THAT MY GOALS ARE USELESS.
WELL PEOPLE ARE USELESS! I MIGHT BE HAPPY IF I COULD ONLY BECOME A...
WHOOPS
DENTIST!!!

RRRR!!!
THUD!!!
NEVER MIND...
FRANK ORANGEVILLE?
YA?
YOU'RE iN LUCK... THERE'S A JOB OPENNING AT BRAND "X", THE COMPANY I WORK FOR... AND I THINK THAT YOU WOULD DO NICELY.
FFFT!!! FFFT!!!
WHAAA?...
HOW WOULD YOU LIKE TO BE IMMORTAL? A CROSS BETWEEN A DENTIST AND A DEMON.
i'D SELL MY SOUL FOR A CHANCE LiKE THAT! I'M SICKA BEIN' HUMAN.
SERIOUSLY?... CAN YOU SEE WHERE THIS IS GOING?

I HOPE THAT YOU WILL ENJOY TAKING OVER THE POSITION OF TOOTHFAIRY!!!
HA!!! HA!!!
HA!!!
OH MY GOD!!!
SNAP!!!
CRACKLE!!!
POP!!!
OH YOUR GOD. WHAT?!

HUMAN PROBLEM
MY TU-TU !!!
WELL I'M AN X-HUMAN. THAT'S CLOSE ENOGH. STICKIN' MY BENT OUTTA SHAPE NOSE INTO THIS DILEMA IS JUSTIFIED!

THE OVAL OFFICE...
ZOINK!!!
WHAT IN THE FREE WORLD?!
Hi, MR. PRESIDENT!!!
ALLA' THIS GREASE IS EFFECTING MY BRAIN AND MY CHOLESTEROL!
LOOKY HERE, BUDDY... WE GOTTA TALK. THE EARTH WILL SOON BE CONTINENT DEEP IN KA-KA IF YOU DON'T ACT FAST.
WAIT A SECOND... WHO THE HAPPY MEAL ARE YOU, YOU... BIG... BAD... MAN?!...
I LOVE HOW YOU EXTRAPOLATE ON THE DETAILS... So ARTiCULATE. BUT TO ANSWER YOUR QUESTION...
THiS PANEL BROUGHT TO YOU BY CLINTON BURGER AND BILL'S FRIES!!!

I'M THE TOOTHFAIRY, HAPPY?
HOW'S THAT?
POW!
PROVE IT, YOU OVERSIZED CREAMPUFF!
I AM SATISFIED AT THIS TIME.

IN DEEP SH... SPACE... LIGHT JUST A FEW YEARS FROM EARTH...
INSIDE AN ALIEN SPACESHIP... FILLED WITH ALIENS... ALIENS FROM A BAD 50's SCI-FI FLICK...
POP!!!
COSMIC PENAL COLONY IN SIGHT, SIR.
DON'T WORRY MR. PRESIDENT. THEY CAN'T SEE US.
OH... HOW VERY DICKENS OF YOU.
HUMANS ARE THE DISGUARDED UNDESIRABLES FROM OUR SUPERIOR ALIEN SOCIETY. THOUSANDS OF YEARS AGO, WE GATHERED ALL OF OUR SICK, USELESS AND EVIL PEOPLE AND DEPOSITED THEM ONTO EARTH...

EARTH ACTED AS A COSMIC PENAL COLONY WHERE WE HOPED THAT ALL OF OUR SOCIETIE'S FILTH WOULD UNWITTINGLY DESTROY THEMSELVES.
WE HAD DECIDED THAT THIS WAS THE BEST SOLUTION BECAUSE WE WERE STRIVING TO BE PERFECT AND WE DIDN'T HAVE THE HEART TO OBLITERATE EVERYONE. BUT INSTEAD OF KILLING EACHOTHER OFF... EARTH HAS PREVAILED, SURPASSING INTOLERABLE LEVELS OF TECHNOLOGY.
?!
*&$$!!!@? %$##@**
WE NEVER THOUGHT THAT HUMANS WOULD EVEN FIND THE AMERICAS BUT THEY HAVE EXCEEDED TO THE POINT OF SPACE TRAVEL AND NUCLEAR CAPABILITY.
SO FOR OUR OWN GOOD WE'RE JUST GONNA HAVE TO KILL THEM... AHHH, WHAT CAN YA DO?
WHY AM I THINKING OUT LOUD AS IF I WAS AN ACTOR ON A SOAP OPERA? WELL, NO MATTER... IT'S A GOOD THING THAT NO IMPORTANT, HUMAN FIGUREHEAD IS LISTENING.

POOF!!!
BACK IN THE LOVE DUNGEON. UHHH... I MEAN OVAL OFFICE!...
THE FINAL PENAL COLONY SHUTTLE HAS JUST BEEN LAUNCHED AND IS HEADED TO THE MOON AS WE SPEAK!
DON'T YOU SEE THE IRONY!?!
HUH?
I WAS HOPING FOR SOME REALIZATION.
HUH?

HELL...
WHEN THE EARTH IS DESTROYED, A NEW, LARGER MARKET WILL OPEN!
THE SUPERIOR ALIENS WILL CEASE TO BE PERFECT AND EXPERIENCE SELFISHNESS, VANITY AND ALL OF THOSE OTHER GREAT HIGH MARK-UP ITEMS FOUND IN HELL'S CATALOGUE!
TAKE A LOSS?...
... TO MAKE A PROFIT!...
CAPTURING SOULS FOR DUMMIES
EVIL!!!

EARTH...
I WOULD LIKE TO ANNOUNCE THAT WE HAVE SUCCESSFULLY COMPLETED RIDDING THE WORLD OF EVERYTHING THAT IS WRONG!
LOOK UP THERE!
OH MY GOSH!
WHAT IN THE HELL IS THAT?
IT AIN'T ELVIS.
LET'S PANIC!

WELL PUT ME INA' BROTHELESS TOWN AND CALL ME UNLUCKY!
RUN FOR YOU LIFE!
SWEET GEE-ZUS!

GULP!!!
HEH, HEH...
WITHIN A FEW MINUTES THE DIPLOMATS ARE ALL REASSEMBLED...
OH MY GOODNESS GREACIOUSNESS!!!
CNN
DOES SIZE MATTER?
WHAT THE HELL IS THAT THING?!... AND WHERE DID IT COME FROM?!
HOW IN HEAVENS NAME SHOULD WE KNOW?
I NEED PRESIDENTIAL BRAIN FOOD. QUICK, SOMEBODY GET ME SOME DORITOS!

ANNOYING FAX NOISE!!!
SIR! SIR! WE'RE RECEIVING A FAX!
A FAX?!
YES SIR. IT'S SIGNED, THE ALIENS!!!
CRUNCH! CRUNCH! CRUNCH!!!
PREPARE TO DIE... PLEASE... SINCERELY, THE ALIENS...
I DON'T THINK SO, YOU DAMN ALIENS! I'M PREPARED! THE TOOTHFAIRY WAS RIGHT! THAT WAS NO ACID FLASHBLACK... 'CAUSE I WAS JUST A POT HEAD!
I DIDN'T JUST MENTION THE TOOTHFAIRY'S NAME OUT LOUD?... DID I?!

3... 2... 1...
KA-POW!!
BANG!!
CRASH!!
BOOM!!
ADAM WEST!!

NA NA NAH
BOO BOO!!!
DITTO!!!
SNIFF!!!
SOB!!!
@!$&*#

THE BIG GUY RELAXED AND LIT A CIGARETTE, A DIVINE CIGARETTE. THE SMOKE CRADLED THE ASHES OF THE EARTH AND THE BONES OF IT'S DWELLERS. THE ENTIRE TWENTIETH CENTURY WAS ALMOST A COMPLETE RIGHT OFF FOR THE AGENTS OF HEAVEN. HELL HAD SUCCESSFULLY CORNERED MOST OF THE HUMAN SOUL MARKET, AND ALTHOUGH THEY DID NOT OWN EVERYONE... THEY BLOODY WELL WOULD HAVE.
SO THE BIG GUY HAD ALL OF THE EVIL PEOPLE OF EARTH SENT TO THE MOON, WHERE THEY WERE KEPT ALIVE, THAT WAY HELL WOULDN'T BE ABLE TO CASH IN ON THEM. SOULS ARE THE EQUIVALENT OF CELESTIAL POKER CHIPS, AND THERE IS A NEVER ENDING, COSMIC GAME OF POKER BEING PLAYED BETWEEN HEAVEN AND HELL.
BIG GUY HAD ALL OF THE GOOD PEOPLE OF EARTH MURDERED VIA THE ALIENS AND THEN COLLECTED ALL OF THEIR SOULS...
THAT WAY, HE WAS PLAYING WITH A BETTER HAND THEN THE DEVIL. THE BIG GUY WAS BLUFFING FOR ALMOST AN ENTIRE CENTURY AND LUCIFER NOW KNEW IT. BY MURDERING EVERY GOOD PERSON ON EARTH, HE HAD JUST PULLED A PAIR OF ACES OUT OF HIS TOGA.
THE BIG GUY WON THE TWENTIETH CENTURY. THE DEVIL PONDERED THE IRONY.

SATAN SAYS, "THE END!!!"

HAPPY PREDATOR PUBLICATIONS

HAPPY NICK'S

FRED the POSSESSED FLOWER

12

"THOSE DAMN CHINESE!"

GUEST STARRING: GOD & SATAN

HAPPY NICK'S
FReD the POSSeSSeD FLOWeR
"THOSE DAMN CHINESE!!!"
WE ALL NEED SOME AFFIRMATION FOR ALL OF THE BUMPY TWISTS AND TURNS AND GENERALLY CRAPPY EVENTS IN OUR LIVES... THERE IS SOME SORT OF SELF-SAFETY MECHANISM IN LOOKING DOWN ON PEOPLE OF DIFFERENT PERSUASIONS. RACE, REGION, SEXUAL ORIENTATION... WHO CARES? LET'S JUST BLAME THE MEAN AND IGNORANT! THEY COME IN EVERY FLAVOR AND THERE IS AN ABUNDANCE OF THEM. IRONICALLY, IT IS MEAN AND IGNORANT OF US TO PAINT MINORITIES WITH THE SAME, PERVERBIAL BRUSH... EXCEPT MIMES! WE ALL KNOW THAT MIMES ARE EVIL! KILL, KILL, KILL! DEATH TO ALL MIMES!!!
Creator, Writer Illustrator, HAPPY NICK

THEY HAVE NO FORSIGHT... NO FAITH! THEY ARE ALL PESSIMISTIC, FACETIOUS SKEPTICS... DON'T YOU AGREE, BOO BOO?!
MEOWWW!
BUT WHAT DO THEY KNOW?! WE'RE CLOSE, BOO BOO... VERY CLOSE!
MEOWWW?
THEY WON'T BE LAUGHING ONCE I DEMONSTRATE MY CREATION!
FFFT!!! FFFT!!!
ASIDE FROM TESLA, DEVICI AND A FEW OTHER GUYS... I!!!... PROFESSOR JON JON VON RESO, HAVE INVENTED THE WORLD'S FIRST TIME MACHINE!!!

TIME CONTINUUM REGULATER, TIME FLUX CALCULATOR, CABIN PRESSURE, EMITIONS SCALE, FUEL, AM, FM, CD, AC, LIFE SUPPORT MONITOR... CHECK.
PRRRR!
NOW THE ONLY THING LEFT TO DO IS TO TEST IT OUT! WISH US LUCK, BOO BOO.
HERE WE GO!!!
ZOOM!!!

HELL... UNDER CONSTRUCTION...
HELL OF FAME
OPENING SOON!!!
i DON'T UNDERSTAND... WE'VE LANDED, BUT THE TIME FLUX CALCULATOR INDICATES THAT WE ARE STILL AT THE SAME TIME VORTEX IN WHICH WE STARTED. LET'S GO AND TAKE A LOOK.
ALITTLE TO THE LEFT, CHARLY!
WHAT THE?...
HEY BOSS, THEY'RE EARLY.

THE GUY WHO WAS RESPONSIBLE FOR PRODUCING GREASE #2.
GREAT, JUST WHAT I NEED.
LOOK... I DON'T MIND IF THE FATE DEPARTMENT WANTS TO OVER SEE THE SPECS ON EVERY LAST COSMIC BUILDING CODE...
THIS THING WAYS A TON!
BUT I...
JUST HANG ON A SEC... YOU GO AND TELL THE BOYS BACK IN PURGATORY TO SHOW A LITTLE PROFESSIONALISM AND BOOK AN APPOINTMENT INSTEAD OF JUST SHOWING UP. UNANNOUNCED!
HSSSSSS!!!

THAT WAS CLOSE, BOO BOO! POSSESSED FLOWERS?! WHAT'LL THEY THINK OF NEXT? A DEVIL WITH A BOW TIE AND BUCK TEETH! NO WAIT... A DEITY WITH A PRISON TATOO! HEH- HEH, WOULDN'T THAT BE PECULIAR?
I'VE MADE SOME ADJUSTMENTS... LET'S TRY LANDING AGAIN.
MEOWWW?
CHITTY! CHITTY! BANG! BANG!
THAT BIG LIVINGROOM IN THE SKY...
OH MY GOD!!!
FFFT!!! FFFT!!!
THAT'S MY NAME, DON'T WEAR IT OUT, OR USE IT IN A BLASPHEMOUS CONTEXT!
HEAVEN'S GATE
YOU COSMIC CABLE GUYS ARE MORE EFFICIENT THEN I THOUGHT. I WASN'T EXPECTING YOU FOR ANOTHER HOUR.
CLICK!!! CLICK!!!
DITTO!

MY DAMN, DIVINE TV IS ON THE 'FRITZ AGAIN. AND YOU'D BETTER FIX IT RIGHT... I PUT THE FEAR OF GOD INTO PEOPLE FOR A REASON, YOU KNOW!
NOW CHOP, CHOP!
DOINK!!!
YA!!!
AND NO FUNNY BUSINESS.
GULP!!!
YUK!!! YUK!!! YUK!!!
I CAN'T BELIEVE THAT THEY ALL FELL FOR THE OLD, "LOOK OUT, SATAN'S BEHIND YOU!!!"
MEOWWW.

WHAAA?!
KABOKI!
BODA!
JACKIE CHAN!
LOOK OUT!!!
BY THE WAY, THIS IS DEATH.

I'M A DEAD MAN!!! PARDON THE PUN.
THIS ISN'T GONNA BE PRETTY!
AS YOU TURN THE PAGE... IMAGINE A LOUD, BONE CRUNCHING, FIBERGLASS DENTING SORT OF NOISE.

MINUTES LATER... THE PURGATORY PARAMEDICS ARRIVE ON THE SCENE...
KA-CHHH!!!
KA-CHHH!!!
WAY TO GO DUMB ASS. YOU KILLED DEATH!
MEDIC
KA-CHHH!!!
KA-CHHH!!!
THE OTHER THREE HORSEMEN ARE GONNA BE PISSED!
DOA
THOSE CHINESE GUYS HAD BETTER STAY THE HELL AWAY FROM ME!
DAMN CHINESE!!!

BACK ON EARTH. SOON AFTER THE DEATH OF AHHH... DEATH.
IT'S GETTING PRETTY BACKED UP DOWN THERE. WHAT THE HELL ARE WE GONNA DO?
HOW IN HEAVEN'S NAME SHOULD I KNOW?

FATE'S COURTROOM...
THE FIRST SANCTIONED CELESTIAL ASSEMBLY OF ALL OF THE COSMIC CORPORATIONS WILL NOW COMENSE.
AS FIRST ORDER OF BUSINESS, I AM INSTATING COSMIC MARTIAL LAW FOR ALL OF THE CIVILIANS RESIDING IN HEAVEN, HELL AND PURGARTOY. THIS WILL STAY IN EFFECT UNTIL WE CAN REPLACE DEATH.
IT WASN'T MY FAULT!... SOME CHINESE GUYS WERE IN THE MIDDLE OF THE ROAD! I WAS TRYING NOT TO HIT THEM!
DAMN CHINESE!!!

WE MUST DISCUSS THIS DILEMMA IN ORDER TO FIND A SOLUTION. NAHHH... LET'S JUST LYNCH THIS GOOFBALL!
HORSE MEN
DON'T PLAY INNOCENT, SCIENCE BOY! WHEN I'M DONE WITH YOU, YOUR BIG BRAIN WILL BE ABOUT AS USELESS AS A TV STATION IN AMISHVILLE!
MIKE
PESTILANCE
FAMINE
TIME
CAN I WATCH?!
I SHOULD START PRAYING... BUT THAT JUST DOESN'T SEEM APPLICABLE.

DIE!!!
DIE!!!
DIE!!!
I MOTION THAT WE HOLD OFF ON WHACKING THIS GEEK. LET'S TRAIN HIM TO REPLACE DEATH INSTEAD.
ALRIGHTY THEN?

HOLY GRAIL
BAR & BILLIARDS
SOMEWHERE IN LIMBO... THE LOCAL HANG-OUT AND WATERING HOLE FOR ALL FREELANCE DEMONS ALIKE...
WHAT DO YOU GUYS THINK ABOUT UPPER MANAGEMENT GIVING THAT DORKY SCIENTIST, VON RESO, DEATH'S JOB?
IT'S ONE HELL OF A PROMOTION ALRIGHT! BURP!!!
WOULD ANY OF YOU PARA NORMAL PEA BRAINS CARE TO MAKE A LITTLE WAGER AS TO THE SUCCESS OF DEATH'S REPLACEMENT?

LIMBO'S WAITINGROOM...
DEATH'S BEDS
LOOK FATE... WE NEED DEATH'S REPLACEMENT IN THE FIELD, ASAP!!! HEAVEN AND HELL ARE GETTING SWAMPED WITH COMPLAINT LETTERS FROM THE DECEASED!...
THERE'S MORE AND MORE COMING IN BY THE CELESTIAL TON.
AND THAT'S NOT EVEN COUNTING THE ONES THAT THE BURNING HEDGE HAS ACCIDENTALLY TORCHED!
NOT ANOTHER STACK!

ON THE JOB, TRAINING...
OK NOW... REMEMBER, YOUR DEATH, NOBODY CAN MESS WITH YOU. BUT HE'S A BIG SUCKER, SO HIT'IM LOW, AND HIT'IM HARD!
FORGET ALL OF THAT TURN THE OTHER CHEEK CRAP! THINK LOCUS', THINK PLAGUE, THINK 100 CHANNELS AND THERE'S NOT A DAMN THING ON!
GRRR!!!
I'LL TRY TO MAKE THIS AS QUICK AND PAINLESS AS POSSIBLE.
YOU BOYS KNOW THE RULES...
DEATH, YOU CAN USE ANY DIRTY, IRONIC TACTIC THAT YOU WANT... AND MIKE, YOUR INTIMIDATING, ANGELIC OPPONENT HAS TO TRY AND PREVAIL.

DING!!! DING!!!
KEEP YOUR GUARD UP!!!
BAM!
USE A FOREIGN OBJECT!... PEARL HARBOUR HIM!!!
MEOUCH!!!

?!
VON RESO...
I MEAN DEATH...
BUDDY? ARE YOU OK?
SAY SOMETHING!
I AM A TOILET ELF.
PUT ME IN YOUR SALAD
AND MARINADE MY
MOTHER-IN-LAW.
TALK ABOUT
CHEATING DEATH.

GAINING WORK EXPERIENCE... IN THE REAL WORLD...
YOU HAVE GOT TO GET SOME HANDS-ON 'CAUSE TIME IS OF THE FREAKIN' ESSENSE! SO FLY DOWN INTO THE CITY AND KILL SOMETHING!
WE HAVE FAITH IN YOU.
SHMUCK.
DEATH #1
DEATH #1
THIS DOESN'T SEEM SO BAD.
?!
HOLY SH... MOKES WE'RE HIGH UP.

BRUCE LEE-
SENSE...TINGLING.
CRACK!!!
PAINFUL-SENSE...
TINGLING!

DAMN CHINESE!!!
HE'S ABOUT AS INCOHERENT AS A STERN LISTENER.

THE LORD SAYS THAT YOU HAVE TO BELIEVE IN YOURSELF, DAMN IT!
FOR THE DEATH OF YOU! USE YOUR IMAGIN-ATION!
I DON'T FEEL RIGHT TAKING PEOPLE'S LIVES...
SERIOUSLY?... ALRIGHT, I'VE HAD IT UP TO MY PETALS WITH YOU! NO MORE MR. NICEFLOWER! IF YOU DON'T KILL SOMETHING RIGHT THIS SECOND, PUNKASS!... I'M GONNA KILL YOU... REPEATEDLY!!!
GULP!!!

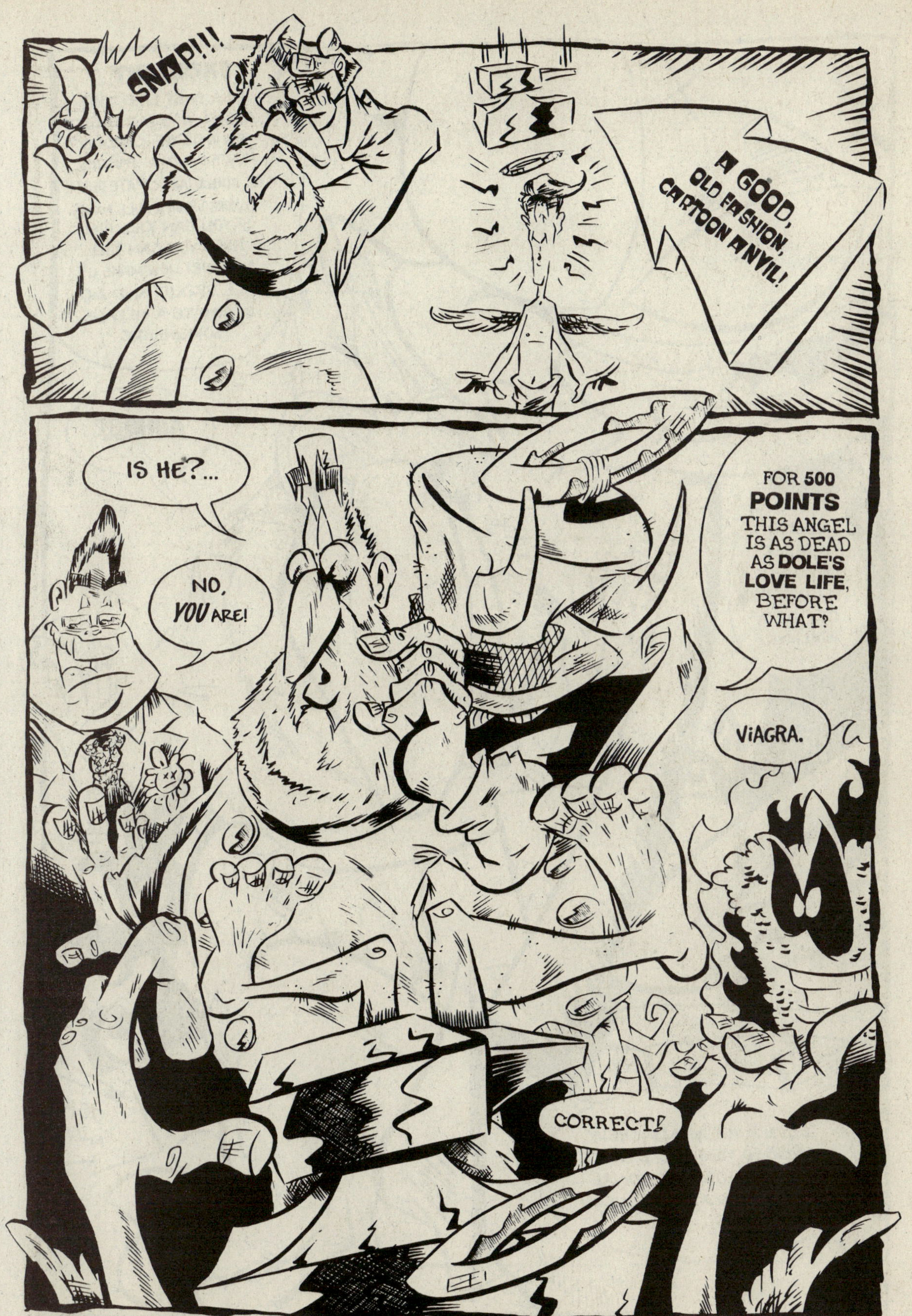
SNAP!!!
A GOOD, OLD FASHION, CARTOON ANVIL!
IS HE?...
NO, YOU ARE!
FOR 500 POINTS THIS ANGEL IS AS DEAD AS DOLE'S LOVE LIFE, BEFORE WHAT?
VIAGRA.
CORRECT!

EXCELLENT!...
IN A PAST LIFE, THIS ANGEL WAS AN ENSIGN ON ONE OF CAPTAIN KIRK'S LANDING PARTIES... HE COULD ANTICIPATE DEATH COMING FROM A MILE AWAY! IF YOU CAN KILL HIM, THEN YOU CAN KILL ANYONE! NOW MAKE US ALL PROUD AND GO DECIMATE A VILLAGE SOMEWHERE...
AHHH!!!
SEND A STOCK BROKER PLUMMETING OFF OF A HIGH RISE...
BETTER YET, WHACK CHEVY CHASE SO THAT THERE WON'T BE ANYMORE NATIONAL LAMPOON VACATION SEQUELS!
DEAD ANGEL♥

I THOUGHT THAT I WOULDN'T BE ABLE TO LIVE WITH MYSELF IF I ACTUALLY WENT THROUGH WITH IT! BUT THIS IS GREAT!... SO REFRESHING!... I LOVE IT!
KILL!!!
KILL!!!
KILL!!!
HEH-HEH.
WHAT A PLEASANT SURPRISE.
IT'S A FACT OF LIFE. EVERYONE DIES! LENNON, BLIND MELON AND OLD BLUE EYES!
ALWAYS ILL-TIMED, AND ALWAYS TRAGIC! FAREWELL MR. HARTMAN, SEE YA' SOON, MAGIC!
DEATH IS A NECESSARY EVIL, DON'T YOU SEE?! SO GOOD BY MAYOR BONO AND JYD!
GOOOO, DEATH!!!

COSMIC BUSINESS HAS PICKED BACK UP...
HEAVEN ARRIVALS
HELL DEPARTURES
PURGATORY DELAYS
PLEASE HAVE YOUR TICKETS READY.
PLEASE BUCKLE UP ALL OF YOUR HOPE AND KEEP YOUR FEAR IN THE UPRIGHT POSITION... YOU MAY STORE ALL OF YOUR CARRY-ON DEBAUCHERY IN THE OVERHEAD COMPARTMENTS.
THANK YOU FOR FLYING GREY MATTER.

THE CELESTIAL ASSEMBLY IS NOW BACK IN SESSION.
DEATH HAS TAKEN A GREAT TOLL ON THE, AHH?... DEATH TOLL. SO I AM LIFTING MARSHAL LAW FROM ALL COSMIC CORPERATIONS.
THE NUMBERS ARE WAY UP! THIS NEW DEATH IS A FREAK!
I LOVE IT!!!
TUTE!!!
TUTE!!!
AMEN!!!
IT IS GREAT THAT HEAVEN, HELL AND PURGATORY FINALLY WORKED TOGETHER, INSTEAD OF COMPETING. WHY DON'T WE MERGE ALL OF THE COSMIC CORPORATIONS TOGETHER AND FORM A MONOPOLY?! YA' KNOW, LIKE ONE BIG, HAPPY FAMILY!!!

BEAT IT, YA' SHMUCK! YOUR GOING TO HELL IN A FLOWER BASKET!
PUNT!!!
YEEOWWW!!!

BACK INSIDE THE HOLY GRAIL BAR & BILLIARDS...
ANTI UP, BOYS! I'M FEELIN' LUCKY TONIGHT! MOMMA NEEDS A NEW FUR COAT!
U CAN'T PH**K WITH MOTHER NATURE!!!
SAY MOMMA SAW MOMMA MA COUSAAA! SUBTITLE: MOTHER NATURE ALWAYS PREVAILS.
SHE ALWAYS WINS!
WHO'S BIG IDEA WAS IT TO LET MOTHER NATURE IN ON THE POOL, ANYWAY?!
I'M NOT A'SCARED A'YOU! BURP!!!

DEATH DELIVERY
30 MINUTES OR FREE!!!
FOR AWHILE THERE IT LOOKED LIKE HEAVEN AND HELL WERE GOING TO GO BELLY UP! AND THAT HUMANS WOULD BECOME IMMORTAL..
BUT REST ASSURED...EVERYTHING IS BACK TO NORMAL, THANKS TO THE NEW DEATH AND HIS SIDEKICK, "BAD LUCK" Boo Boo. SO DON'T WORRY, YOU WILL ALL STILL, EVENTUALLY DIE HIDEOUSLY.
CATS RULE.
ON A LIGHTER NOTE... THERE WAS A MISTAKE IN THE BETTING POOL, SO MOTHER NATURE HAD TO GIVE HER WINNINGS TO THE RIGHTFUL VICTORS. THOSE...
calm before the storm
DAMN CHINESE!!!
SIANAURA!!!

A GRAPHIC NOVEL BY H.N. HARDCASTLE

WINTER 2000

HAPPY PREDATOR PUBLICATIONS
HAPPY NICK'S
FRED the POSSESSED FLOWER
13
"AN AUTUMN LIFE IN NAZI LAND"
665
664
GUEST STARRING: GOD & SATAN

HAPPY NICK'S

FRED the POSSESSED FLOWER

in

"AN AUTUMN LIFE IN NAZI LAND"

HELLO ALL...

WE ARE NOW SOMEWHERE BETWEEN *LIFE* AND *DEATH*... PERHAPS NOWHERE?... PERHAPS HELL...

TODAY WE WILL WITNESS THE FATE OF YOUR PRECIOUS, LITTLE PLANET FROM THE SAFE PROXIMATY OF AN *ALTERNATIVE DIMENSION.*

THIS *DEVIATED REALITY* HAS EVERYWHERE ON *EARTH* TRAPPED UNDER *NAZI REGIME,* WITH THE EXCEPTION OF RUSSIA... THE ONLY FREE COUNTRY STILL IN EXISTANCE.

HITLER STILL RULES DECADES LATER, IN PRESENT DAY... AS HIS BRAIN HAS BEEN PRESERVED THANKS TO THE ALWAYS ADVANCING TECHNOLOGIES OF THE GERMAN AUTOMOTIVE INDUSTRY.

IN THIS DIMENSION *HITLER* DID ***NOT*** INVADE RUSSIA, MAKING THAT *FATAL, NAPOLEONIC MISTAKE* WHICH COST HIM **WWII.**

PRESENT DAY...
Von Coke
VON PEPZY
OK OK.. TWO RABBIS AND ZA RED BARON WALK INTO A BAR..
I ZINK I HEARD ZIS ONE.

IN ZA FAZZA LAND...
OH MY DARLING DAUGHTER AND HEAD GENERAL OF MY ARMIES, BECKY SUE!!!... TODAY IS A GLORIOUS DAY TO BE A NAZI! EVER SINCE WWII, RUSSIA HAS ELUDED NAZI RULE, THWARTING MY PLANS FOR COMPLETE DOMINATION OF THE WORLD. BUT NOW WE HAVE FOUND A WAY TO DESTROY RUSSIA! THERE BY NAZIFING THE PLANET 100%, MAKING IT FIT FOR YOU TO INHERIT.
THANKS DADDY!
TO EXPLAIN HOW WE WILL ACCOMPLISH ZIS NARCISSISTIC, ARION TASK IS MY OWN PERSONAL, MAD SCIENTIST, ZA YELLOW SNOW!!!
BECKY SUE?!
I WAS GOING TO CALL MYSELF, MR. FRUZE AND SHOOT PEOPLE WITH A FROZEN YOGOURT GUN... BUT THE YELLOW SNOW GIMIC SEEMED SO MUCH MORE OMINUS!
HITLER-IN-A-BOWL!
DUMKOFF.

ZA LABORITORY...
RUSSIA'S TREACHEROUS, SNOWY LANDSCAPE HAS ALWAYS BEEN A MAJOR FACTOR IN OUR FAILED ATTEMPTS AT INVADING. BUT I HAVE CREATED A MACHINE THAT WILL TURN THEIR STRENGTH INTO THEIR DOWNFALL!
BY USING AN ELECTROMONTUBULATOR CONNECTED TO A BARIMETRIC PANTAMIDER, WE CAN VELOSITATE THE ATMOSPHERIC PRESSURE AND ENVELOPE RUSSIA, VODKA DEEP IN CRYSTALISED, AMBER H2O!!!
VON HUH?!
IN LAYMAN'S TERMS... WE'LL BUILD A GIANT YELLOW SNOW MAKER AND BURY RUSSIA FOR GOOD!
YA!!! NOW ZAT SOUNDS GOOD!

THIS PARTICULAR SITUATION EFFECTS US IN THE COSMIC SECTOR ALITTLE DUBIOUSLY...
UP UNTIL NOW, HEAVEN HAS BEEN IN THE LEAD, RAKING PEOPLE'S SOULS IN BY THE CELESTIAL TRUCKLOAD
YOU SEE... HEAVEN IS FOR THE NAZI REGIME. AS LONG AS THE WORLD IS IN CRISIS, PEOPLE WILL SHOW UNITY AND HOPE. TYRANNY MAKES PRAYERS A DAILY HABBIT.
AS FOR HELL... THEY WANT FASCISM TO CRUMBLE 'CAUSE THE MORE FREEDOM YOU HAVE, THE MORE SELFISH, TAKE FOR GRANTED, CUT-THROAT, MANIPULATIVE DEBAUCHERY WILL FLOURISH!
GREEDY CAPITALISTS!
COUNT'EM, FIVE LEAVES.
AT FIRST GLANCE ALL OF THIS MIGHT SEEM BLASPHEMOUS AND SICK... BUT TRY TO SEE THE BIGGER PICTURE. YOU KNOW... ALTERIOR MOTIVES AND ALL THAT!

HOW ABOUT SOME SHOOTING PRACTICE, HEINRICH?
YOU CAN TAKE OUR LIVES, BUT YOU CAN'T TAKE OUR FREEDOM!!!... GAAK!!!
WHATEVER YOU SAY, SWINE. HEH!!! HEH!!!
BLAM! BLAM! BLAM!

HEAVEN'S
COMPANY DIRECTORY
CONGLOMERATE: CHRISTIANITY & ISLAM
NOVELTY: JOHOVAH'S WITNESS & SOCCER
CULT: SCIENTOLOGY
NONSUBSCRIBER: ATHIEST & SATANIST
HELLO, MY NAME IS: MIKE
HELLO, EVERYONE. MY NAME IS MIKE AS YOU CAN SEE FROM MY CLEARLY MARKED NAME TAG. I'LL BE YOUR ANGEL THIS EVENING SO IF ANY OF YOU HAVE ANY QUESTIONS, FEEL FREE TO ASK.
SEE WHAT FROD MEANS ABOUT RAKIN'EM IN?...
PLEASE HAVE YOUR HOLY REDEMPTION VOUCHERS READY AS YOU ENTER YOUR RELIGIOUS HOME ROOMS.

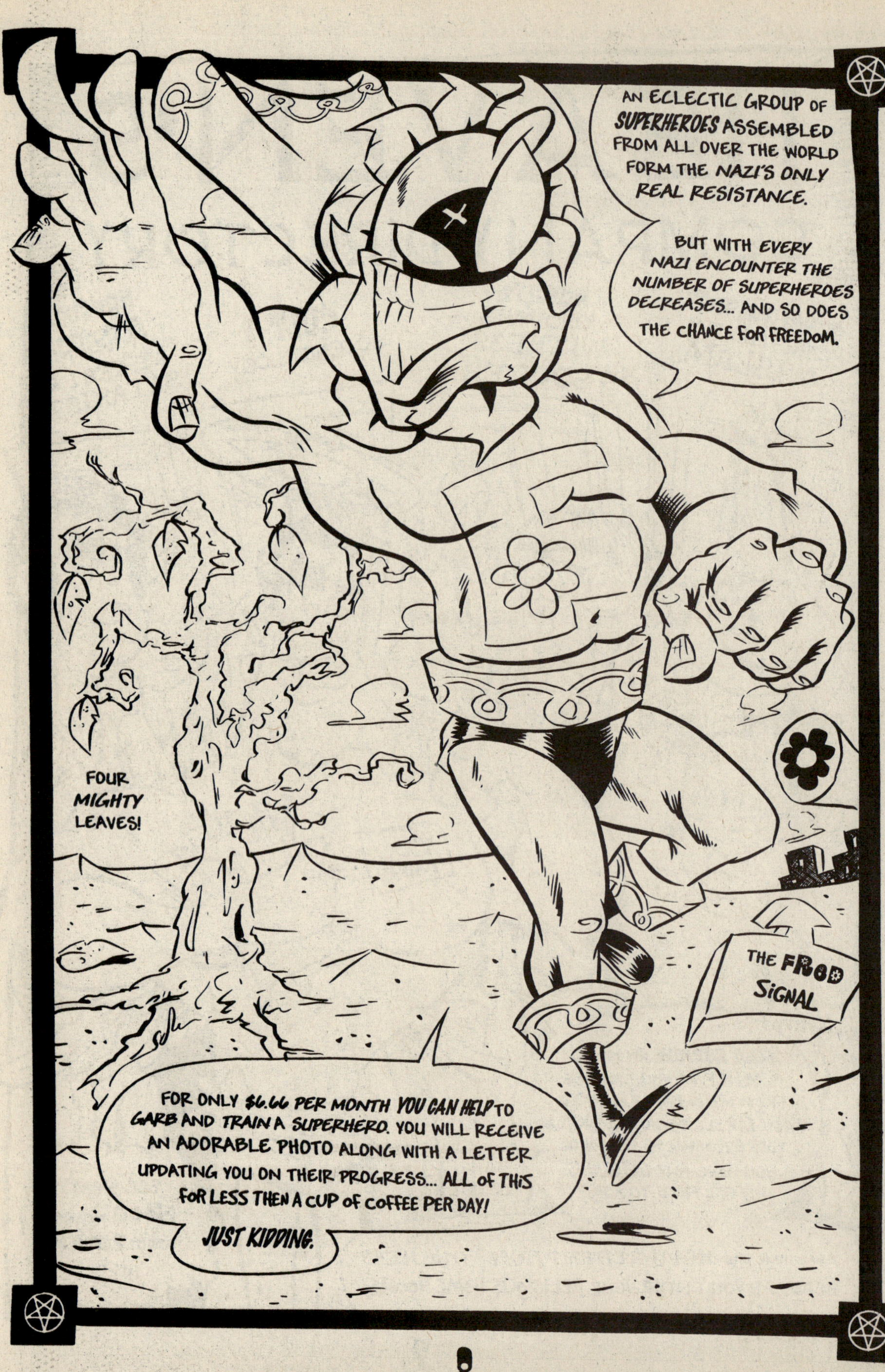
AN ECLECTIC GROUP OF SUPERHEROES ASSEMBLED FROM ALL OVER THE WORLD FORM THE NAZI'S ONLY REAL RESISTANCE.
BUT WITH EVERY NAZI ENCOUNTER THE NUMBER OF SUPERHEROES DECREASES... AND SO DOES THE CHANCE FOR FREEDOM.
FOUR MIGHTY LEAVES!
THE FROD SIGNAL
FOR ONLY $6.66 PER MONTH YOU CAN HELP TO GARB AND TRAIN A SUPERHERO. YOU WILL RECEIVE AN ADORABLE PHOTO ALONG WITH A LETTER UPDATING YOU ON THEIR PROGRESS... ALL OF THIS FOR LESS THEN A CUP OF COFFEE PER DAY!
JUST KIDDING.

TAE KWON DON!!!
BLAM!
BLAM!
BLAM!
GREEN ACRE!!!
FLATULANTEY!
BLAM!
BLAM!
BLAM!
UNSOLICITED MAN!!!
FART!
BLAM!
BLAM!
BLAM!
AUSTA LA VISTA, BABIES!

THE N.S.G.E.
THE NON-PROFIT SUPERHEROES GUILD OF EARTH!
DON'T MESS WITH THE HUMAN PORCH!!! PORCH ON!
THIS LOOKS LIKE A JOB FOR... HOW YOU SAY?... BROKEN ENGLISH MAN!!!
I'M THE RUSSIAN PRIME MINISTER AND THE LEADER OF THE N.S.G.E.... THE RED TAPE!!!
I'M THE RHINESTONE MENNONITE!!! AND THIS IS MY TRUSTY, EAST INDIAN SIDEKICK, SHEESH KABOOB!!!
RIGHT BOSS!

I'M ONLY HAPPY WHEN THERE'S VIOLENCE TO BE HAD 'CAUSE I'M THE GAY BASHER!!!
WIPING THE STREETS CLEAN OF CRIME AND FLUSHING THE CRIMINAL ELEMENT OUT OF SOCIETY... I'M ENMA LAD!!!
BEHOLD, MR. SUPERCALA-FRAJULISTIC!!! I HATE INJUSTICE, ESSPECIALLY FAT INJUSTICE!
EACH MEMBER IS ELBOW DEEP IN SUPERPOWERS AND COMES COMPLETE WITH THEIR OWN SPECIFIC ART DIRECTION!

INSIDE THE SECRET HEADQUARTERS OF THE N.S.G.E.... SOMEWHERE IN RUSSIA..
WE MUST ACT FAST! IF THE NAZIS USE THE YELLOW SNOWMAKER TO COVER RUSSIA WITH AN ICE CAP...
NOT ONLY WILL FREEDOM BE LOST BUT THE WORLD WILL ACCIDENTALLY FALL INTO ANOTHER ICE AGE, WHICH WILL IN TURN CAUSE THE EXTINCTION OF ALL LIFE ON EARTH!
THE RED TAPE IS RIGHT! TOO MUCH GROSS, YELLOW STUFF WILL BE LETHAL... TRUST ME, I KNOW!
LET'S JUST ATTACK'EM HEAD ON! THE NAZIS WON'T EXPECT US TO BE THAT STUPID! KILL!!! KILL!!! KILL!!!
YOU HAVE GOT WAY TOO MUCH CAFFINE IN YOUR DIET, MR.

NO MATTER WHAT HEAVEN AND HELL'S POSITION IS ON THE TOPIC OF FASCISM VS FREEDOM... BOTH INSTITUTIONS REALISE THAT IF THE NAZIS DESTROY RUSSIA, THEY WILL UNWITTINGLY CAUSE THE END OF THE WORLD AS WE KNOW IT.
THEN, THE MARKET FOR REDEEMING AND DAMNING SOULS WOULD DRY UP... FORCING BOTH CELESTIAL COMPANIES TO GO COSMICALLY BANKRUPT!
LEAF x 3
HEAVEN AND HELL, NOW HAVE A MUTUAL DILEMMA. HOW WILL THEY ENSURE THAT THEIR FAVORITE SIDE WILL PREVAIL... WITHOUT SENDING EARTH INTO ANOTHER ICE AGE IN THE PROCCESS?

IN THAT BIG LOONEY BIN, UP IN THE SKY...
BURNING HEDGE, HOLY GO-HOST, MIKE... WE MUST COMMANDERE A SCHEME TO PREVENT RUSSIA'S DEMISE, WITH NO ILL EFFECT ON THE NAZIS.
YA!!! NO ILL EFFECT ON THE NAZIS!
I'M JUST GONNA STAND HERE, LOOKIN' PRETTY, AND NOT OFFER ANY IMPUT.
I HAVE AN IDEA, BIG GUY! A PLAN IN WHICH THE REBEL SUPERHEROES WILL MAKE EXCELLENT PAWNS!

HELL'S FLUNKIES... THE BOOGIMAN, TOOTHFAIRY AND CUPID, ALONG WITH HELL'S OWNER AND OFFICIAL SPOKESPERSON, LUCIFER ALL STRESS OVER THE SAME CRAP AS HEAVEN...
WHAT THE HELL ARE WE GONNA DO?! WITH FROD BUSY NARRATING THIS DAMN STORY, WE HAVE TO MAKE ALL OF THE DECISIONS OURSELVES!!!
YA' KNOW WHAT THAT MEANS?...
WE'RE PH**KED!!!
YO YO, SUCKA FOOS! M'GOTTZ ALLDAT ANA BAGGA CHIPS! SUBTITLE: FELLOW COLLEAGUES, I KNOW EXACTLY WHAT TO DO.
WORD TA BIG BIRD! SUCKA, SUCKA CHILL! WORD, YO! YO! SUBTITLE: A ROUSE THAT ENVOLVES MANIPULATION, STRATEGY AND FORTITUDE.

N.S.G.E. SECRET HEADQUARTERS...
THE ONLY WAY TO ATTAIN FREEDOM IS A COU!
BLESS YOU.
THIS IS WHAT WE WILL DO... WE'LL ATTACK THE FATHER LAND AS A DIVERSION...
VIOLENCE, ALRIGHHHHT!!!
WHILE THE NAZIS ARE PREOCCUPIED WITH US, THE RHINESTONE MENNONITE SHEESH KABOOB WILL SNEAK INTO THE ARMORY AND SABOTAGE THE YELLOW SNOWMAKER.
ARE YA' UP TO IT, SHEESH?
NO PROBLEM, BOSS.

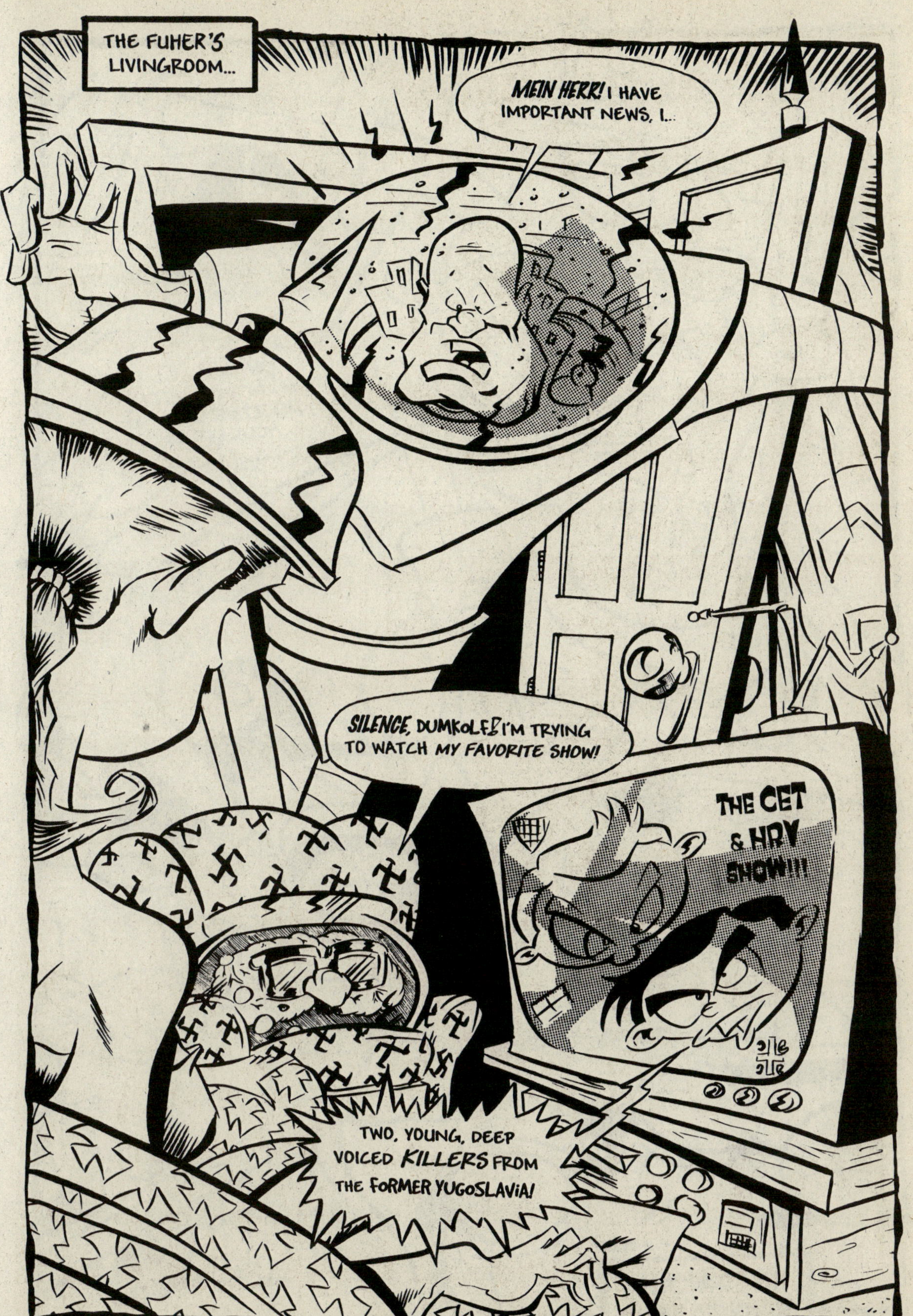
THE FUHER'S LIVINGROOM...
MEIN HERR! I HAVE IMPORTANT NEWS, I...
SILENCE, DUMKOLF?! I'M TRYING TO WATCH MY FAVORITE SHOW!
THE CET & HRV SHOW!!!
TWO, YOUNG, DEEP VOICED KILLERS FROM THE FORMER YUGOSLAVIA!

MY FATHER CAN OUT SMOKE YOUR FATHER!
OH YA!!! WELL MY FATHER HATES MUSLIMS MORE THEN YOUR FATHER!
THAT'S IT!... NOW YOU DIE!!!
NO!!! NOW YOU DIE!!!
THE ETHNICALLY CLEANSED END!!!

HAW HAW HAW THOSE TWO, CRAZY KIDS CRACK ME UP EVEY TIME.
NOW... WHAT WAS IT ZAT YOU WANTED TO TELL ME, YELLOW SNOW?
THERE ARE RUMORS OF A POSSIBLE SUPERHERO THREAT.
ZA N.S.G.E. MUST BE GETTING DESPARATE AS WE CLOSE IN ON RUSSIA..
IF ZAT IS ZA CASE, THEY COULD VERY WELL BE UP TO NO GOOD.

ZA SUPERHEROES ARE OF NO CONCERN!
ZA YELLOW SNOWMAKER IS FULLY OPPERATIONAL AND IS THE ULTIMATE SOURCE OF DESTRUCTION IN ZA VORLD!!!
I WOULDN'T BE TOO PROUD OF ZIS TECHNOLOGICAL TERROR ZAT YOU'VE CREATED... ZA POWER OF ZA YELLOW SNOWMAKER IS INSIGNIFICANT TO ZA POWER OF ZA FORCE.. EH?... I MEAN ZA FASCISM!!!

DID YOU KNOW THAT HITLER WAS AN ARTIST BEFORE HE EVER GOT INTO POLITICS?... UNFORTUNATELY, HE MADE A MUCH BETTER DICTATOR THEN A PAINTER.
EARTH LOVES HIM, NOT.
PLUCK!!!
JUST TWO FREAKIN' LEAVES LEFT!
IF PEOPLE HAD JUST BOUGHT HIS WORK IN THE FIRST PLACE, MAYBE WE COULD HAVE AVOIDED ALL OF THIS.

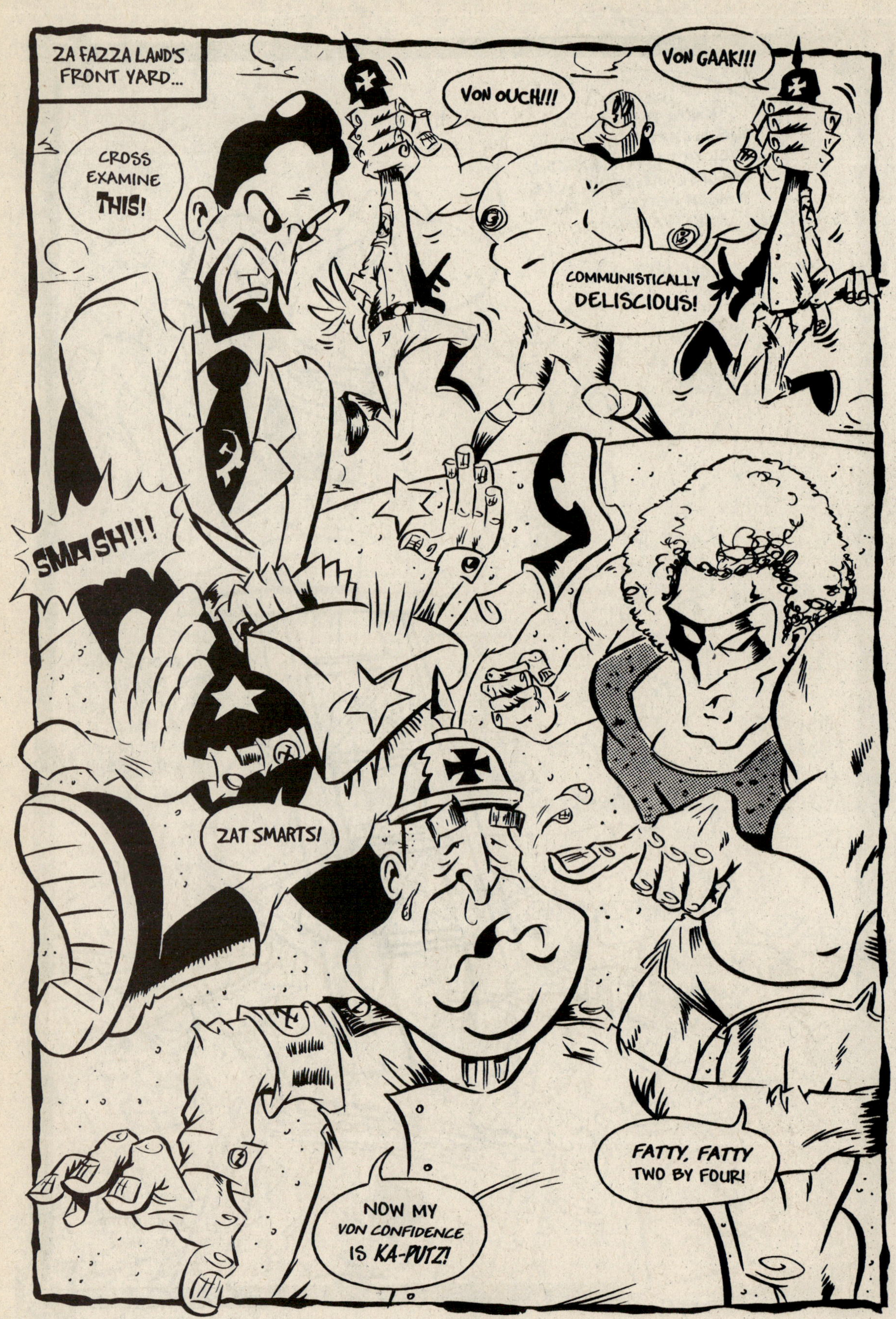
ZA FAZZA LAND'S FRONT YARD...
CROSS EXAMINE THIS!
VON OUCH!!!
VON GAAK!!!
COMMUNISTICALLY DELISCIOUS!
SMASH!!!
ZAT SMARTS!
FATTY, FATTY TWO BY FOUR!
NOW MY VON CONFIDENCE IS KA-PUTZ!

BLAM!!!
BLAM!!!
BLAM!!!
I LEARNED THIS MOVE FROM THE WIZARD'O OZ!
THUD!!!
HOW YOU SAY?... GOING INTO SHOCK AND DYING!
TAKE ZAT.
HEH!!! HEH!!!
SEPTIC TANK'D JUSTICE!!!
KEEP ZAT AWAY FROM MY VON POOP SHOOT!

MEANWHILE... INSIDE THE NAZI ARMORY...
HEH, WHAT'RE YOU DOIN' HERE?
NOTHIN'!
ME NEITHER!
KURRY BOMB
GIANT YELLOW SNOW MAKER
MADE BY A. WEST CO.
THE KURRY BOMB IS READY. WHEN SOMEBODY TURNS THE YELLOW SNOWMAKER ON... KA-POW!!!
GOOD WORK, SHEESH.
THANKS BOSS.

MINUTES LATER...
ZIS IS ZA DAY ZAT ZA NAZIS MONOPOLIZE ZA EARTH!
WHEN YOU HAVE ZA ENERGY AND ZA PERSISTANCE OF A DOZEN POTATO POWERED ALARM CLOCKS, LIKE I DO!... YOU CAN ACCOMPLISH ANYTHING!
ENOUGH ALREADY, DUMKOLF! I'D LIKE TO SEE MY DREAM OF NAZIFYING ZA PLANET DONE TO FRUITION BEFORE I GO TO ZAT BIG BLITZCREIG IN ZA SKY! MY BRAIN CAN ONLY SOAK UP SOME MUCH FORMALDYHIDE, YOU KNOW?
YOU HEARD MY DADDY... MAKE IT SNAPPY!

SOMEWHERE IN RUSSIA...
KREMLIN BURGER
RUSKY'S AUTOBODY
PLEASE, OH PLEASE!.. ANYTHING BUT THE YELLOW SNOW!
DON'T EAT THE YELLOW SNOW!
WHAT'S GONNA HAPPEN TO MY BLUE SUEDE SHOES?!

SUPERHEROES!!!
CLICK!!

IF IT ISN'T MY ARCH ENEMY, THE RED TAPE!
AH, MY ARCH ENEMY, HITLER IN A BOWL!
IT'S OVER HITLER! BY THE WAY... DID I ANNOUNCE THAT YOU ARE MY ARCH ENEMY?... I CAN'T REMEMBER.
ENOUGH OF YOUR RED TAPE, RED TAPE! YOU'RE TOO LATE, THE YELLOW SNOWMAKER HAS ALREADY BEEN ACTIVATED AND RUSSIA WILL SOON BE DESTROYED!!!
IF IT ISN'T MY ARCH ENEMY, MR. SUPERCALAFRAJILSTIC!
AH, MY ARCH ENEMY, BECKY SUE HITLER!
BECKY SUE... HITLER?... I MEAN... IF IT ISN'T MY ARCH ENEMY, THE YELLOW SNOW!
AH, MY ARCH ENEMY, ENIMA LAD!
HOW COME I DON'T GET AN ARCH ENEMY?

THE CREEPY TREE INTERMISSIONS THAT HAVE BEEN PLAGUING THIS STORY ARE BROUGHT TO YOU BY HELLMARK CARDS...
THE COMPANY THAT LET'S PEOPLE KNOW HOW YOU REALLY FEEL...
KARMA POLICE
YOU NEVER KNOW WHAT TWIST OF FATE AWAITS YOU. RIGHT FATE?
TWIST!!! TWIST!!!
HOLY SMOKES! ONE LEAF TO GO.
SERIOUSLY!

MALFUNCTION! MALFUNCTION!
MY BEAUTIFUL CREATION! IT'S GONNA BE ZA DEATH OF US ALL! I'M JUST GONNA GO TO ZA LITTLE TYRANT'S ROOM AND CHECK MY ANTI-FREEZE... I'LL BE BACK!!!
CURSES!!! I WOULD HAVE GOTTEN AWAY WITH IT TOO, IF IT WASN'T FOR YOU PESKY KIDS!... I MEAN, SUPER HEROES!
SO MUCH FOR THE FAMILY BIZ! NOW MY LIFE IS NOTHING BUT A GIANT WONDERBAR, FLOATING IN ZA TOILET! WELL AT LEAST I'M TAKING YOU CAPITALIST SUPERPIGS WITH ME!
I DON'T THINK SO, MEIN HERR.

WE'RE SUPERHEROES, SILLY... WE CAN FLY!
HERE'S SOME LAST MINUTE SALT ON THE WOUND... COURTESY OF EVEYONE THAT YOU HAVE EVER THROWN IN AN OVEN OR IMPALED WITH A BAYONET!
A FLAMING BAG'O DOG SHTUFF!!!
?!
JUST KEEP THAT AWAY FROM MY FRONT DOOR!
PLEASE!!! NOT ZA VON KA-KA!!!

VON BOOM!

DOWN ZA ROAD...
SINCE THE N.S.G.E. HAS DESTROYED THE FASCIST HEAD, THE PERVERBIAL BODY HAS DIED.
WITH HITLER OUT OF THE PICTURE WE GERMANS HAVE A NEW GOAL THAT'S NOT SUPRESSING TOWARDS THE REST OF THE WORLD!...
DUMKOFF.
IT'S OUR GREATEST CHALLENGE EVER! WE'RE WORKING ON OUR SENSE OF HUMOR !!!

#W☉📖✡
!*☠@W
YOU'RE SQUEEZING THE CARBON DIOXIDE OUTTA ME!
HOW WERE WE SUPPOSED TO KNOW THAT HELL SABOTAGED OUR SABOTAGE?!
STILL JUST MINDING MY OWN BUSINESS, AND LOOKIN' GOOD.

OUT OF THE THREE MEAZLY TIMES THAT I'VE APPEARED IN THIS STORY, WHY THE HELL HAVE I BEEN CONTINUOUSLY DRAWN IN THE SAME SIZE AND POSITIONED IN THE SAME CORNER OF THE PAGE? HMMM, HAPPY? IF THAT IS YOUR REAL NAME?!
TO PUT IT IN LAYMAN'S TERMS... HEAVEN JUST WANTED TO BREAK THE YELLOW SNOW MAKER. HELL TOOK THE EXTRA STEP AND CONVERTED THE YELLOW SNOW MAKER INTO A VEHICLE FOR FREEDOM. IN BUSINESS, IT'S ALL ABOUT GOING THE EXTRA STEP.
ORIGIAL THOUGHT: LIFE IS LIKE A BOX OF... WHAT I MEANT TO SAY WAS, LIFE IS LIKE THE WHEATHER... YOU NEVER KNOW WHAT YOU'RE GONNA GET... UNLESS YOU WATCH THE NEWS, BUT TRUST ME, YOU DON'T WANNA WATCH THE NEWS 'CAUSE IT'S ALWAYS BAD STUFF. HOWEVER, IF YOU CLICK THE CHANNEL, YOU MIGHT FIND SOMETHING HALF DECENT... WHERE WAS I GOING WITH THIS, AGAIN?
I CAN'T BELIEVE THAT YOU NAMED YOUR DAUGHTER, BECKY SUE! YOU REALLY ARE A MADMAN!
ALL THE LEAVES GO Bi-Bi...
BRAND "X" BRAIN FOOD
HITLER... BABE... I KNOW THAT YOU'VE BEEN BAD. I ALSO KNOW THAT YOU AND YOUR STUPID LITTLE MUSTACHE ARE ABOUT TO VISIT A PLACE THAT IS SO VILE, THAT THERE IS EVEN CHALK OUTLINES OF COCKROACHES.
YA THINK ZAT I'M SCARED OF YOU?! YOU THINK ZAT I'M SCARED OF YOU?! WELL I DON'T SEE ANY OTHER DEAD DICTATORS SHAKIN' IN THEIR BOWLS, SO I MUST BE SCARED OF YOU!
THE BITTER END

Crank

it DOWN!